JULES MOUNTAIN is a maverick entrepreneur who, having survived an aggressive form of cancer, set himself the task of climbing Everest to prove he was still physically fit. He was at base camp in April 2015 when Nepal suffered its worst earthquake in living memory, and he was buried alive – an experience he recounted in his book *Aftershock* (Eye Books, 2017). He lives in Guernsey.

Praise for *Aftershock*

'The extraordinary story of the man who survived cancer and then attempted to climb Everest, only to find himself in the middle of the deadliest day of the mountain's history'
BBC Radio 5 Live

'The story of the disaster is a remarkable chronicle of resilience and resourcefulness, but also of almost manic determination'
Daily Mail

'Provides a candid, harrowing account of the devastating events of April 2015, when an earthquake provoked avalanches on the world's most famous mountain'
Geographical

'A heart-stopping eyewitness account of Everest's deadliest day in history'
Adventure Travel magazine

ARCTIC INSANITY

4,300 MILES OVER THE POLAR ICECAP BY HELICOPTER

JULES MOUNTAIN

Published in 2025
by Eye Books Ltd
29A Barrow Street
Much Wenlock
Shropshire
TF13 6EN
www.eye-books.com

ISBN: 9781785633928

Copyright © Jules Mountain 2025
Cover by Ifan Bates
Cover image of Bell 505 courtesy of Bell
Map by Simon Edge

Typeset in Palatino Lt Std and Cera Pro

The moral right of the author has been asserted. All rights reserved. No part of this publication may be reproduced, stored in a retrieval system, or transmitted, in any form or by any means without the prior written permission of the publisher, nor be otherwise circulated in any form of binding or cover other than that in which it is published and without a similar condition being imposed on the subsequent purchaser.

British Library Cataloguing in Publication Data
A catalogue record for this book is available from the British Library
Printed and bound by CPI (UK) Ltd, Croydon CR0 4YY

Our authorised representative in the EU for product safety is:
Logos Europe, 9 rue Nicolas Poussin, 17000, La Rochelle, France
contact@logoseurope.eu

CONTENTS

Map	
Prologue	11
1. A Crazy Plan	13
2. Test Flight	26
3. Heading North	39
4. Towards the Back of Beyond	48
5. A Frosty Welcome	53
6. Poor Visibility	61
7. Into the White	74
8. Aborted Mission	83
9. Calling the Police	90
10. Way Too High	108
11. The Red Zone	121
12. On the Polar Ice Cap	134

13. A Bed for the Night	141
14. Party Time	152
15. Facing the Fog	165
16. Between the Clouds	176
17. Flying on Film	189
18. Sunshine in the Faroe Isles	205
19. A Rollercoaster Ride	215
20. Home Straight	223
Acknowledgements	237

For my daughters,
Steph and Lizzie

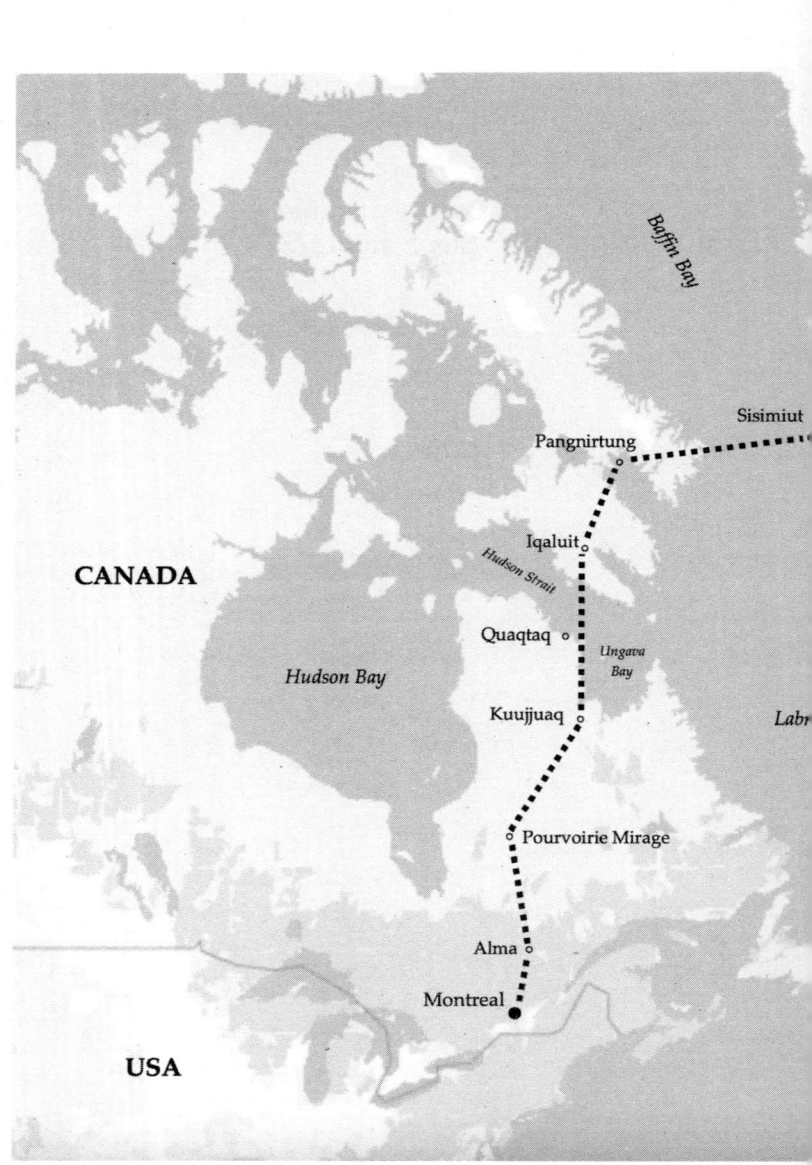

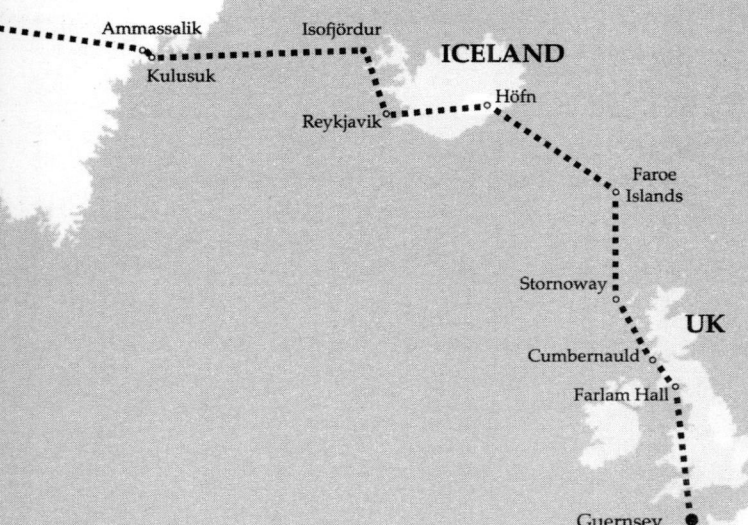

PROLOGUE

'My feet are having a hard time,' said Martin.

Mine were too. The helicopter didn't offer much protection from the elements; there was only a thin layer of plastic and carbon fibre between us and the freezing high-altitude temperatures.

'Turn the heating on,' I said.

Martin reached for the heating knob. There was an ominous crunching sound, after which the knob spun around uselessly. This was not good.

We had no way of knowing if the heater had broken while set on de-fog for the windscreen, or heat for the feet, so now we had no idea if we were going to be able to de-mist the windscreen, or if we would just have hot air pumping onto our feet for the rest of the journey. Keeping warm is important, but being able to see is the main priority, so I prayed it was stuck on de-fog.

'BEEP BEEP BEEP! COLD BATTERY, COLD BATTERY! BEEP BEEP BEEP!'

ARCTIC INSANITY

The warning light blinked angrily on the screen. Shit! What now? Beside me, in his co-pilot's seat, Martin had turned as white as the clouds below us.

I realised what was happening. The outside temperature was minus 14°C, and had been for the past three hours. The aircraft had probably never been tested to these sorts of extremes before and it was not happy. I knew how it felt.

I had no idea whether the helicopter had been designed to fly at these temperatures for periods as long as we had been flying up there – around three hours – but I *did* know it was designed to fly for a maximum of only three hours at a time. And even though our extended-range tank enabled us to fly it for five hours straight, maybe that would not hold up in such crazily cold conditions.

Those conditions certainly seemed to be taking their toll: the computer system was basically packing up. We had a broken heating control, ECU degrade and a frozen battery. And to top it all I was running low on wine gums.

'BEEP BEEP BEEP!' went the helicopter warning system again. This was the third warning.

That was it, we were surely going to die. We were done. Toast. Heading for the icy waters of the sea.

1
A CRAZY PLAN

Just before Christmas in 2019 a friend phoned me at my house in Guernsey to say that he was buying a Bell 505X single-engine helicopter, which was being built in Canada.

He explained that potential buyers visit the Bell factory in Quebec, Canada, and take a flight in the helicopter. If they decide to buy the machine, it's dismantled, placed in a shipping container, loaded onto a ship and transported across the Atlantic. When it arrives in the UK, it's re-assembled and flight-tested again. Only then do you have your shiny new aircraft.

'But it's all phenomenally expensive,' he said.

A crazy thought hit me. 'How about we cut out the middleman?'

'What do you mean?'

'I'll fly it back for you.'

He let out a guffaw. 'You're joking, aren't you?'

'I'm serious.'

'Jules, don't be stupid. You can't fly a helicopter from Canada to the UK.'

'Why not?'

I believe that if you stay in your comfort zone your whole life, you waste your potential.

'It's too far. That's why.'

'But it must be possible.'

'Has anyone ever attempted it before?'

'No idea.'

Better to die trying than never to have tried at all, I thought to myself. I would rather live a very full life and hope I make it to old age than sit in my wheelchair dribbling into my tea dreaming about all the things I wish I'd done.

'I doubt it. I mean, helicopters like the 505X aren't designed to fly those sorts of distances.'

'Yeah, but I'd make some stops.'

'But you'd have to fly very high over a frozen landscape. It's treacherous. It's not like flying across the Home Counties.'

'I get that.'

'Do you? You'd be flying across some of the remotest areas on the planet.'

'That's part of the challenge.' I wanted to test myself as a pilot and see how good I really was. 'Come on, then, will you let me do it?'

The more I thought about it, the more I liked the

idea. The trip would be an opportunity to raise some more money for the charity I support, the haematology cancer care unit at University College, London. Several years earlier, I'd been diagnosed with cancer just as I was about to sell my second management consultancy, and had to have a tumour removed from my head. I almost died. So the charity is very close to my heart.

'You really want to do this, don't you?'

'It would be fun.'

'You know, anything could go wrong. You'd need to do your homework well.'

'Don't worry, mate, I will.'

I'm not a novice when it comes to adventure. I had actually been to the Arctic before, on a ski-touring and dog-sledging expedition, when we took a commercial flight to Iceland and then continued on a smaller plane to Kulusuk, on the eastern coast of Greenland. I had also climbed Everest. That involved a massive logistical challenge. I've always considered myself good at meticulous planning: it all comes down to knowledge, resourcefulness and adaptability. That expedition pushed me to the limit, which was precisely what I wanted when I chose to undertake it. Mind you, no amount of planning, or equipment, can guarantee you will be safe. Weather is unpredictable. I nearly got killed in an avalanche triggered by an earthquake in Nepal.

'What if you run out of fuel?'

'I'll make sure I don't.'

'You might crash.'

'I could have an accident walking down the high street.'

'I know you like a challenge, Jules, but, if I'm honest, I think you're crazy.'

I laughed. 'Maybe I am.'

'Only you could come up with such a hare-brained idea.'

Maybe he had a point, I thought when I came off the phone. What had I done? Exactly the same as I had done when I vowed to climb Everest. After Everest, I said I'd go to the North Pole, but my heart wasn't in that. I kept telling people it was next on the agenda simply because everybody kept asking what I was going to do next. Flying a helicopter from Canada across the Arctic Circle to the UK excited me, though. It was exactly the kind of challenge I'd been looking for.

I'd first caught the helicopter bug in the summer of 2017 when I took my two daughters, Steph and Lizzie, to the Hertfordshire Country Show at Redbourn, near the farm where I then lived. As we wandered through the crowds, I came across a guy at one of the stands who was demonstrating a microlight aircraft. It was basically a cloth wing with a lawn-mower engine strapped to it. I stood watching him with growing fascination.

A CRAZY PLAN

'This thing is amazing,' I said to him.

'It is, isn't it?' he replied proudly.

'What do you need to do to be able to fly one?'

'Just twenty-five hours' flying time.'

'Is that all?'

'Yeah. And then you're good to go.'

I was amazed; this was incredible. Twenty-five hours and I could get airborne in a microlight. I could whizz around the farm and have some fun. You know when something lights a fire inside you? I have to do this, I thought to myself. The seed was sown.

I then heard the immortal words, 'Dad, I'm bored,' and my daughters dragged me away from the stall to go shopping in the crafts marquee. I love my daughters to bits.

At that stage, that was the extent of my plans: take off from the back field, whizz around in the skies above Hertfordshire for a little while, then drop back down into the field. Great fun, I thought.

As soon as I got home that evening, I googled everything I could about microlights. I found out you could get a one- or a two-seater, but that was about it. That was your limit. It would be fun, but I wanted to share the experience with my family. It's very important to do things you enjoy with somebody else – to share the adventure. I'd learnt that from skiing: nice by yourself, but great with your girlfriend or a bunch of mates. I didn't mind being up there in the sky alone, but I would much sooner have company.

Within an hour of starting my research, microlights were shelved and I'd moved on to helicopters. I found out that Harrison Ford flies one – and a jet helicopter at that. Having played Han Solo in *Star Wars*, he has now become the character.

Helicopters aren't as simple as microlights. You need 11 exams and a minimum of 45 hours of flying to qualify, but by now I was hooked on the idea. I signed up to train as a pilot.

It proved to be seriously tough work. In truth, there were many occasions when I very nearly gave up. You control a helicopter with what's called a cyclic stick, located between your legs. You push it forward to go forward, back to go back, left to go left, and right to go right. If you keep moving the cyclic in a circle, the aircraft doesn't know where to go, so it should stay still. It does work, but if you do a big stir, the machine rolls all over the place while remaining in the same spot. Trying to hover five feet above the ground is incredibly difficult. There is a reason why more people learn to fly light planes than helicopters.

With my instructor sitting beside me, we'd be going forwards relatively steadily. I would move the cyclic slightly to the left and we'd lurch like we were on a rollercoaster. I'd overcompensate – swing it back to the right – and two seconds later we'd lurch back to the right. One time, the instructor said to me, 'If you don't stop all this lurching, you're going to make me sick.' It was all I could do to keep the machine in the air, let alone control it. Gradually, I came to understand the subtleties involved. The cyclic is incredibly sensitive and you only need to move it very slightly: almost like you're mind-controlling the helicopter.

Four gruelling months later, on a nerve-racking day in November, dripping with perspiration after a two-and-a-half-hour flight with the examiner right next to me, I gained my wings – my helicopter pilot's licence. It was a wonderful moment.

'What do people usually do after they pass?' I asked.

'They stick their licence in their bedside drawer, and it never comes out again,' my instructor replied.

For most people, that really does seem to be what happens. They don't fly for a month, then they leave it for another month – maybe the weather is bad, maybe they're busy. Another month goes by. Suddenly it's three months later and you've got to go in and do an hour-long check flight before you can rent an aircraft to go somewhere. They can't really be bothered. Six months go by. They're out of practice; then they're basically done.

I could see how easy it would be to fall into this trap with work, kids and so on, but I swore to myself, there and then, that my licence would not die quietly in any drawer. I promised I would do at least an hour's flying every month to keep myself sharp. I'd hire a Robinson

R22, the tiny two-seater helicopter I had qualified in, and do a trip up to Derbyshire to see my dad. I'd find excuses to go somewhere, do something, get up in the air. Eventually, I bought a Bell 206 Jetranger, on the recommendation of my instructor, and made frequent trips from Guernsey, where I was by then living, to the mainland. With each trip, I became more skilled and confident.

When I began to plan the trip from Canada to the UK, I soon realised I couldn't fly in a straight line across the Atlantic – that way I'd run out of fuel and very soon drop into the soup. I'd have to hop northwards up through Canada to Greenland, across the polar ice cap and then on to Iceland, before hitting the Faroe Isles, followed eventually by Scotland and finally down to Guernsey. The thought of the sights I'd see from the air – the stunning scenery of northern Canada's massive forests, Greenland's vast ice expanses and the polar ice cap, Iceland's amazing fjords and volcanoes and the Faroe Isles' legendary mist (perhaps I wasn't looking forward to that quite so much) – made this an astonishing opportunity. I became obsessed with the idea.

I worked out that the flight from Canada to Guernsey would be around 4,300 miles – compared with about 3,000 miles on the most direct route, which a 747 transatlantic flight would take – and I could probably

A CRAZY PLAN

do it in ten days. The Bell 505 has a range of just under 300 nautical miles at 4,000ft, so I'd be pushing the machine to its limits, while also fighting the elements at down to minus 15°C.

Figuring out the logistics for a trip like this was complicated, to say the least. One of the most important things was working out all the fuel stops. The helicopter has a standard fuel tank for three hours' flying. That meant I needed an airport within two and a half hours' flying time from each stop. In the UK, about every 50 miles there's another airfield and an opportunity to land and refuel every 50 miles or so, mostly because of the hundreds of small airfields that sprang up during the Second World War and still exist today. It's extraordinary: if you pin them all on the map, the country looks like a pincushion of airfields. Canada was a very different case. The further north you go, the tiny settlements are a long way apart.

I also had to make sure that after 25 hours flying I could arrange a service and check, which was tricky, as I couldn't say for sure where I would be. And I might have to turn back at any stage during the trip because of severe weather.

On top of all this, in these incredibly remote areas, I had to find places to sleep at each overnight stop and ensure that the helicopter had a valid registration number, airworthiness certificate, insurance and radio certificate. And I was flying over territories that involved all kinds of bureaucracy just to set my craft down. I lost count of the number of phone calls I made to the Danish Embassy in London to get permission to land in Greenland and the Faroe Isles (territories owned by Denmark).

I also reluctantly conceded that I needed a co-pilot. It wouldn't be wise to attempt this kind of journey flying solo. This was my crazy idean and I very much wantd to fly the helicopter the whole way, but I couldn't ignore the fact that an experienced co-pilot would be an essential ingredient of the trip, providing general moral and practical support in such dangerous terrain, and available to take over if I became too tired to fly.

I immediately thought of Martin, a pilot who had flown a helicopter in Greenland for researchers doing work about the polar ice cap, and who lived in Northern Ireland. I'd been introduced to him by the cravat-wearing Quentin Smith, known as Captain Q, whom I'd met at Denham Aerodrome in Buckinghamshire, where he was managing director and chief flying instructor at a helicopter hire and maintenance company. Quentin was world helicopter champion twice and the first person to fly to both the North and South Pole in a single engine helicopter, so I took his recommendations seriously. I hadn't met Martin in person, but we'd had a number of Zoom calls to discuss various aspects of flying. Familiar with the freezing terrain we would be crossing and with some of the extreme weather conditions we might encounter, he would be the perfect co-pilot.

I duly phoned Martin and put the idea to him, explaining all the practical stuff. Would he think I was nuts too? Fortunately, he relished the challenge, just as I did. By the end of the call, I had persuaded him to accompany me on the adventure.

In the middle of my preparations, along came Covid-19, with all the restrictions and testing that varied from country to country. I had to make sure that Martin and I complied with everything that was required in a fast-changing situation. Even for me, who prided myself on my logistic skills, it threatened to be overwhelming.

Somehow, though, I got everything done. One evening in early June 2020, I arrived at Heathrow Airport to catch a flight to Paris, where I would change for a flight to Montreal. (I'd arranged to meet Martin in Canada.) I made my way through the crowds towards my check-in desk at Terminal 4, feeling worried. I had an aircraft transceiver and a satellite transceiver, as well as my mobile phone, in my backpack. It looked so dodgy: the sort of stuff I imagined a terrorist might need. But without it, the trip was off, as there would be no way to navigate or communicate from the helicopter.

My hold luggage was also a concern. I was carrying a large plastic expedition bag chock-full of strange items

I'd need on my trip. When flying over Greenland, due to its remoteness, any aircraft needs to have a lot of emergency equipment on board as a legal requirement. This includes: life jackets; life raft; first aid kit; tent; compass; paraffin cooker; and – strangely – a piece of string of unspecified length. Presumably so you can do a bit of ice fishing, but that mystery was never solved. If we were stopped for any reason and we didn't have all those items on board, we'd be grounded instantly, either by the Canadian authorities or the Danes.

I was especially concerned about the turtle pack, a collapsible extra fuel tank that would increase the distance the helicopter could fly in one go. I'd cleaned it out as thoroughly as I could and wrapped it very tightly in plastic bags, but it still had the distinctive aroma of jet fuel. It also had two motors attached and a load of wires. This pack was utterly essential because some of the sea crossings – from Northern Canada to Greenland, or Greenland to Iceland – would push the helicopter to its upper fuel-capacity limits. If anything went wrong – if we had to turn around or fly in a strong head wind – we seriously risked running out of fuel.

We also needed to have eight flares on board, but even I wasn't crazy enough to try to get these through customs in my hand luggage. After many attempts, I'd managed to order them online in Canada to be sent straight to the hotel I'd booked in Montreal.

Nevertheless, all the other stuff I was carrying filled

A CRAZY PLAN

me with anxiety as I joined the queue at the security checkpoint. I placed my backpack in the grey tray and watched as it inched along the conveyor belt towards the X-ray machine. I stepped through the scanner, feeling sure that I would be taken to one side and questioned. But, to my surprise, no one said anything. It was the same at Charles de Gaulle Airport. I was just waved through, like all the other passengers. I could scarcely believe it – though obviously I wasn't complaining.

Settling into my seat on the Air Canada 747 for the eight-hour flight to Montreal, I realised that there was no turning back now. I was about to embark on an adventure. It was risky, I was well aware. But I was ready for the challenge of putting the flying skills I had learned to the test.

2
TEST FLIGHT

I landed in Montreal early in the morning and waited anxiously by the carousel, watching the bags and suitcases tumble onto the conveyer belt. If my hold luggage didn't come off the plane, the trip was scuppered. After what seemed like ages, but was probably only a few minutes, to my relief, it arrived. I lugged it outside to find a taxi to take me into the centre of the city.

At my hotel, I freshened up in my room and popped down to the restaurant for breakfast. A couple of hours later a limo from Bell arrived outside the hotel to take me to the company's factory in Mirabel, a half-hour drive north.

The Bell site occupies a vast area, containing seventeen helipads and two runways. For anyone who loves helicopters, Bell is the place to visit. The company was founded in New York in 1935 to design and build fighter aircraft. It built the first US fighter jet and then starting making helicopters, producing thousands for the Vietnam war.

I entered the reception in the main building, remembering to rub my hands with sanitiser from the plastic bottle on a stand. Catherine Emond, the client relationship manager, was waiting to meet me. I showed her my Covid certificate from the test I had taken at the hotel.

'That's all fine,' she said from behind her face mask.

'I've been excited about coming here,' I said, gazing around me.

'So you're planning to fly one of our 505Xs all the way to Europe?' Even behind her mask, I could see her look of incredulity.

'That's the idea.'

'I don't think that's ever been done before.'

'So I've heard.'

I asked how many 505Xs the company had made.

'Around two hundred,' Catherine said. 'Something like that, anyway. The model was unveiled in 2013 and we delivered our first one in 2017, if I remember correctly.'

'So I might be the first person to really put it through its paces.'

'If you're going to fly it to Europe, then I'd say you definitely are.'

We walked behind reception and down a long

corridor, past many offices, and came to the huge workshops at the back of the building. On the assembly lines were helicopters at various stages of production. I was in my element, and I pulled out my phone to take some pictures.

'Sorry, no pictures, Jules,' said Catherine. Bell is very sensitive about its processes, she explained, especially as it also builds military helicopters. I was disappointed not to be able to share pictures with my engineering buddies, but I understood the reason. It was privilege enough to receive this fabulous shop-floor tour.

I'm a chartered engineer and I've worked in large factories like this, but I'm still always amazed at the technology and skills of the workers. Conversely, the other remarkable thing is that, however complicated these incredible machines may be, when you break them down into their component parts everything is actually quite simple.

As Catherine walked me around, I watched some workers wiring a partially assembled Bell 407, and others working on windscreens, creating the perfect curve to fit the machines. Every element of the helicopter production line was on show. To see these things exposed like skeletons as the engineers tinkered away behind the panelling, pulling together all the critical elements to produce a working aircraft, was incredible. With helicopters, the skill is in working out how to make those components fit together in such a

TEST FLIGHT

way that the craft is still light enough to get into the air, and has blades tough enough not to fall to pieces under the pressure they're subjected to. I could have spent weeks there, loving every minute of it. I was in awe of Bell and the seriously talented individuals who work for the company.

But Catherine had another treat in store. 'I guess you'd like to see your 505X,' she said.

'You bet,' I said.

She escorted me to the far end of the hangar, where a red curtain hung from the roof to the floor.

'This is it,' she said, and flicked a switch.

The curtain opened to reveal the most beautiful, polished, gleaming white helicopter sitting on a

The unveiling of the 505 in the factory – what a beautiful machine!

moveable helipad. It looked simultaneously delicate and powerful. The main cockpit was framed by a large Perspex window, a bubble that allowed a nearly 180-degree view. The two blades above the cockpit hung limply, belying their potential to spin at 500rpm just two feet above the pilot's head. The tail extended from the rear of the main body of the aircraft, looking sleek and sharp.

I peered inside the cockpit, which was reassuringly uncomplicated, because it was computer-controlled; it looked nothing like the 206 Jetranger I was used to flying. There were five cream leather seats, two in the front and three at the back. They smelled like the premium Italian leather in a new car, and I took a long, slow indulgent sniff. The two front seats each had cyclic and dual controls, as well as foot pedals, with the magnificent FADEC (Full Authority Digital Engine Control) dual computer screen system placed between them. This controlled the engines during start-up, while they're running and at shutdown, making the process much quicker. The 206 didn't have any of that.

We were joined by a Bell test pilot in a brown all-in-one flying suit, whom Catherine introduced as Mathieu Asselin. He walked me around the aircraft, pointing out various details and running a finger over the navigation system. He then connected the external power supply, switched on the FADEC computer system and started to take me through all the set-up options.

'The 505's currently configured for the American and Canadian market,' he explained. 'When you get to Europe, you'll need to take it to a workshop to get it reconfigured.'

This was news to me. 'How long will that take?'

'A couple of days, that's all. It's pretty simple. Now, there is one final thing we must do.'

'What's that?'

'The test flight.'

I watched as the hangar doors behind the helicopter opened and it was gently manoeuvred outside, across the runway, to a small helipad surrounded by grass.

I was suddenly nervous. Here I was, at the holy grail home of helicopters, with only three years' flying experience under my belt, surrounded by people who lived and breathed these machines, and I was to test-fly this spectacular one.

'Right then,' Mathieu said. 'Let's do it.'

As we left the hangar and walked outside to the take-off point, I dug out my habitual old England rugby cap and aviator sunglasses (both essential when flying a helicopter into the sun to stop blinding) from my bag. Putting them on, I instantly felt more confident; I'd done this quite a few times, in another 505 in which I had been practising in the UK. I just needed to follow the same process as I always did.

I got into the cockpit with Terry, my co-pilot for the

test. I plugged in the four-point harness and grabbed the laminate check list I'd brought with me from Guernsey. It's easy to forget something, so use the list, I told myself. Check the instruments, check the fuel, run all the engine tests and emergency checks. Radio frequency set; direction indicator, altimeter set. I didn't want to look like a muppet in front of these professionals. It was all perfect and we were ready to go.

I turned the start button. This machine is extraordinary because once that button is turned, the computer takes over and engages the blades and fires everything up. It's only if something goes wrong that you have to manually override the computer and shut everything down. The turbine engine can reach 870°C on start-up, so it's vital not to let it overheat. And boy, that is hot – and just two feet above my head!

The blades began to turn, lazily at first, as the whir of the turbines increased in pitch. I watched the dials like a hawk in case I needed to shut down. But everything was running smoothly and soon the blades were up to idle speed. At that point I just had to wait for the transmission and engine oil to warm up and the sensors to show green on the computer screen.

Once the oil was up to temperature, there was one more button to press to go from 'idle' to 'fly'. This is where the blades really speed up (383rpm), so it was time to hang on to all the controls, both feet and both hands engaged. I pressed the button and heard the whine of the turbine as the blades increased in speed dramatically and became a blur above my head. I felt the helicopter becoming light on the skids.

At that moment the power lever was fully down. When I lifted it, we would become airborne. This is a lovely moment you get to experience as a helicopter pilot – the delicate moment when the skids of the helicopter you're commanding leave the ground, and the helicopter twitches with power. No matter how many times I take off, that exhilaration never seems to dampen. But as I took off in the new 505, which had only flown for three hours in its whole life, I felt a special kick of adrenaline. What if they hadn't tested it properly? What if something failed? You hear about this all the time with car manufacturers – a recall to fix a defective part – with the difference that here, when a part fails, we might be 2,000ft up in the air. I felt a lump in my throat.

I pulled the power lever and the helicopter rose smoothly upwards into the sky.

Terry made a radio call and then said, 'OK, Jules, let's climb to 2,000ft and head north.'

'Wow, this is fantastic!' I said, looking down at the Bell factory below.

After we had been flying for about 20 minutes, Terry said, 'How about an ILS landing?'

'You're kidding me. This thing has ILS?'

'It certainly does.'

ILS stands for Instrument Landing System, a radio navigation system that provides short-range guidance to allow aircraft to approach a runway at night or in bad weather, such as fog. This is pretty fancy stuff.

'Let's do it.'

Sure enough, we returned to the Bell factory landing strip under ILS. It was a remarkable experience, as the computer picked up the ground height and the runway and I just watched the screen and kept the helicopter between the two lines on it, like playing a computer game. Amazingly, there was no need to see anything out of the window. It made me wonder what other fabulous features this machine had that I didn't know about.

The test flight was over and I was dazzled. The only problem we thought we had found was with the heater in the cabin – one setting didn't seem to work. The factory engineers had the nose cone off in a jiffy and checked it all over. It was fine.

I strolled around the aircraft, tested out all the controls, and made sure everything felt right, double-checking to be sure. I was being extra-cautious, but for good reason: the aircraft was about to go on a 4,300-mile trip, which would involve around 70 hours of flying time, after previously having barely been flown. If anything rattled loose on the trip, that would be the end of Martin and me.

Eventually I told Catherine I was happy with everything. She took me to a conference room to sign all the various documents for the sale and registration of the helicopter.

That done, I sat down at a long table in the conference room with Mathieu to discuss the route. If there's anything that really gets a helicopter pilot going, it's discussing routes. I wondered if he thought I was crazy to attempt such a long and difficult flight.

'This is it,' I said to Mathieu, flipping open my laptop and showing him the points I'd plotted out on SkyDemon, the flight planning and navigation software I used in the helicopter in the UK. I hoped they would allow us to fly up into the far north of Canada ready for our hopping-off point to Greenland. I had planned a direct route north and then picked out fuelling points roughly every 400 miles. A bit like driving a car, except there are far more petrol stations for cars. The line of the route was straight up, then zigzagging to pick up the fuel stations. It was only a rough plan, because I didn't know Canada and I'd never flown in the country. I had very little concrete information about what would be waiting for us when we dropped down into these remote parts of the world without warning, in temperatures of minus 15°C. I was hoping for a lot of luck.

Mathieu looked at the route carefully, his brow furrowed. It was like an examiner studying my work.

An eternity passed before he took a deep breath.

'The route's no good,' he said.

My heart sank.

My plan, once we'd taken off from Montreal, was to head to Robertval or Alma, then to a place called Renard Diamond Mine. It was in the perfect spot, on a line going directly north. I admit, I was also a little excited about the prospect of visiting a diamond mine; I had visions of getting to take a little look around, if not at the actual mine, at least at its entrance. I had already rung Renard mining company to ask permission to land. They had turned down my request but I thought perhaps Bell could swing it for me.

'They'll say no,' said Mathieu. 'And there is nothing we can do here at Bell to persuade them. Due to Covid, a lot of places in the northern territories are letting their fuel stocks run down and they won't let visitors stop or refuel.'

I'd expected difficulties with stitching together a route on other sections of this trip, but I hadn't anticipated Canada being such a problem.

'What do you suggest?' I asked.

He pointed out a tiny fishing village called Pourvoirie Mirage. I'd never heard of it – never even seen it on SkyDemon – but there it was.

'You won't have a problem there,' said Mathieu.

'They'll be able to refuel me?'

'I'm pretty certain. There's a small dirt runway for

incoming fishermen. Let's go through the rest of the route and I'll phone them to make sure.'

We sat there for a couple of very animated hours, rejigging the route together and phoning remote airfields to check if they had jet fuel and were happy for me to land.

I was amazed by how helpful Mathieu was being with something that was really not part of Bell's remit. I was truly impressed by the company – not only for their splendid aircraft but also for going out of their way to ensure their customer enjoyed the experience and got home safely.

I was particularly grateful for Mathieu's support because he was a highly skilled and experienced pilot. To have the benefit of his insight into the Canadian part of my route was a great privilege.

What he didn't tell me as we sat there in the conference room, but I found out later, was that at the time he was talking to me his father was critically ill, by all accounts close to death. But there he was, talking to me with great composure, helping me plot a route through the most remote parts of Canada – a true professional. It was surreal, looking back, although perhaps it actually provided him with a small escape from his painful family reality.

'Right,' he said at last. 'I think we have a route. From here, you fly to the town of Alma, as you planned, then to Pourvoirie Mirage. After that, it's Inuit territory. You fly to Kuujjuaq, then it's your first big ocean crossing: you go over the Hudson Strait to Iqaluit. For the final Canadian leg, you stop at Pangnirtung, then it's a straight line over the fjords, across the sea to Sisimiut in Greenland.'

'Sisimiut?' I said. 'I was planning to head to Nuuk.'

'No, you want to go from Pangnirtung to Sisimiut. With the fuel capacity on the 505, it's a better route. Believe me, you need the crossing to be as short as possible.'

There was no way I was going to argue with him.

I arranged with Catherine to return to the factory at nine in the morning to take the 505 and begin the first stage of our trip. I couldn't wait.

3
HEADING NORTH

Early the following morning, Martin and I took a taxi to the Bell factory. He had arrived late the previous night. Over a couple of beers in the hotel bar, I'd given him an overview of the 505 and outlined the route and stops. Despite his jet lag after the flight from Dublin, he was bubbling with excitement and couldn't wait to get into the air.

However, bad news awaited us at the Bell factory. Catherine told us that the Federal Aviation Administration (FAA) paperwork hadn't come through, meaning the helicopter wasn't registered and therefore not cleared to fly. I should have known this would never really be as simple as turning up, jumping into the helicopter and heading out.

Catherine told us we could make use of the conference room, which had a small kitchen attached, so we could keep ourselves going with cups of tea or coffee. The delay gave Martin and me time to pore over the maps and charts again for the hundredth time, checking and re-checking, trying to work out every permutation of what could go wrong and how we would manage it. There were too many possibilities for us to figure them all out, so luck would need to be on our side.

We spent nearly four hours rearranging the aircraft ahead of the beginning of the expedition. The three back seats had to go to make room for the turtle pack, so we took them out and packed them into a wooden crate to be shipped to Guernsey. We then started packing all our stuff into the helicopter. By that point, I was itching to get away.

The spare fuel tank, and our ability to transfer fuel into the main tank while flying, was still bugging me. The helicopter can fly for three hours on its main tank, but the flight from Canada to Greenland would take four and a half. Even with all our reserve tank fuel, we could only fly for five hours. This gave us only 30 minutes' contingency, which in flying terms is very tight. If we flew into a strong headwind or encountered a problem transferring fuel from the spare tank to the main tank while halfway between Canada and Greenland, it would be too late to turn back, and we wouldn't have enough fuel either to make it to Greenland or to get back to Canada. In other words, if the fuelling system should fail at that point, we would face certain death.

The extra fuelling system relies on a 24-volt pump that plugs into the cigarette lighter, spiking at switch-on to potentially 5 amps, and then pulling 2 amps. The cigarette lighter was fitted with a 5-amp fuse. I was a little concerned, as I'd have my iPad connected with my navigation system, my phone, the satellite phone and the fuel pump, all on a 5-amp fuse.

When you switch on an electrical appliance like a pump, it will spike, so it won't be just 2 amps; it would reach 5 amps or more before settling back down. That could be enough to trip the 5-amp fuse.

The fuses were located behind the luggage compartment, outside the main cockpit. It would be a Tom Cruise manoeuvre to climb outside onto the skids, slide backwards while we were flying, avoid getting my head lopped off by the blades, open the door behind the luggage compartment and try to reset the 5-amp fuse. At 160mph in the freezing cold of the northern regions, it would be pretty much Mission Impossible.

'You know what?' I said to Martin.

'What?'

'I reckon the best thing to do would be to buy two 12-volt batteries and some wire, and link them together to create the 24v needed for the pump.'

He thought about this for a moment, then said, 'Agreed. If the worst came to the worst and the 5-amp fuse tripped, we can hook the pump up to the batteries.'

'Yeah, with a bit of luck they should last long enough to pump enough fuel through to get us across the sea.'

I reflected afterwards that with the longest leg being four and half hours, this was probably wishful thinking. Nevertheless, it seemed to be our best option.

We took a taxi to a large, soulless DIY store, with aisles stretching away as far as the eye could see. As well as the batteries, I picked up a toolkit for the helicopter, including some spanners, a knife and screwdrivers. I was kicking myself all the while, because I'd almost brought a toolkit with me from home, but at the last minute dropped the idea. Now here I was spending money on a toolkit I'd likely not use after this trip.

We returned to the Bell factory. By the end of the day, however, the FAA paperwork still hadn't arrived, despite Catherine's best efforts to chase it up.

We returned the following morning. Still no paperwork. What's more, new obstacles had emerged to delay our getaway. When Martin and I were inspecting the helicopter, a mechanic wandered over.

'There's a bit of a problem,' he said.

My heart sank. 'What?'

'It's mostly software-related.'

'What do you mean?'

'We've got to update the software to the latest version.'

'OK. How long will that take?'

'Anything between one and four days to get it uploaded and working properly.'

I took a deep breath. We were on a strict schedule, with hotels and refuelling booked in various places, and I'd learned from previous expeditions, like Everest, that keeping to schedule was very important; any delays could seriously impact the chances of success. The fact that we hadn't even started yet and were already running three days behind schedule was definitely a cause for concern.

Fortunately, the software issue turned out to be a false alarm: unbeknown to us, the test pilot had updated it already. Then, just before three thirty, there was a knock at the door of the conference room and Catherine entered.

'Good news,' she said excitedly. 'It's all done.'

'Fantastic!' I cried, punching the air.

'When do you want to go?'

'Now?'

'You don't want to wait until tomorrow?'

'I want to get the show on the road.'

'Yeah, let's go,' said Martin.

I was worried that if we delayed until the next morning, by the time we'd arrived at the factory, had a cup of tea and chatted for a while, we wouldn't actually get away until lunchtime.

Also, since the first leg of the trip was relatively short – flight of an hour and 40 minutes from Montreal to

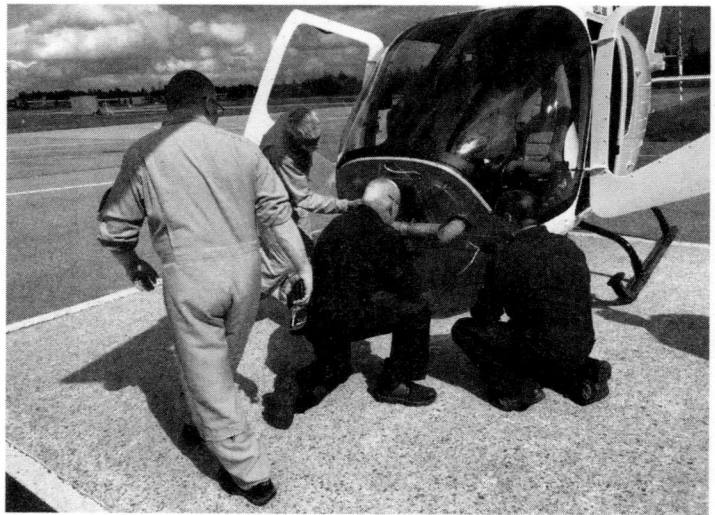
Last-minute adjustments under the nose cone before our departure from Bell

Alma – there was easily time to do it that same day, and at least we would finally be on our way.

We had everything packed and ready to go by 4pm. The factory was beginning to close down, but our corner of it buzzed as we made the final preparations.

Finally, I climbed up into the shiny new helicopter with butterflies in my stomach, tingling in my fingers and incredible excitement. This was it. People came out of the factory to watch us take off – probably wondering whether these two idiots would ever be seen again.

I radioed through to Montréal–Trudeau International Airport to request clearance, which was approved. Then, at last – I pulled the collective lever, which affects the pitch of the blades and therefore the amount of lift they create – and the beautiful shiny white 505 helicopter lifted into the air.

It didn't take long to clear Montreal airspace and leave the city behind. What's amazing in Canada, compared to the UK, is that, once you've cleared the cities, there is virtually nobody out there. In England, there's always a radar station somewhere that you can radio into to ask them if there are any aircraft in your vicinity.

Soon we were simply flying in a straight line across Quebec, without further interaction with the ground. The aircraft handled like a dream – responsive, dynamic and perfectly calibrated. It was the ideal first leg of the journey to get me settled in before the more daunting flights ahead.

After 80 minutes of really enjoyable flying in the sunshine, I glimpsed a vast body of water on the horizon. This was the 400-square-mile Lake Saint-Jean, and it was my cue to radio to Alma, requesting an overnight stay and a refuel.

'You are cleared to land by the fuel pumps. There is no other known traffic to affect you,' crackled the reply.

'On finals.'

I popped the aircraft down right next to the pumps and left the ground team to do its work.

Our plan was to find somewhere to grab some food

and get to bed early so that we would be refreshed for the next day's flying, when I'd really be able to get the miles under my belt and reach the remote north of Canada – while also testing out the helicopter. The first day's flying had been a mad rush to get to Alma, at the same time as adapting to flying in a different country, so I hadn't really been able to focus on the machine or to enjoy the flying – and that's what it's really all about.

I remember I was once out boating with my brother, Rick, and we had just pulled out of Dover into incredibly rough seas. After 20 minutes of going up and down and side to side and feeling very sick, he turned to me and said, 'Jules, this trip is supposed to be fun, and this is not fun.' He was right, so we headed back into Dover and took the train home. I remembered my brother's wise words.

Alma is an attractive small lakeside town with a population of around 30,000. It had no Covid restrictions. We dropped our bags at the motel and walked up the pretty wooden-fronted high street, which felt a bit like something out of the Wild West, until we found a bar at the end of it. It looked out over a grassy common and was heaving with people. The bar was all open-air. It was a lovely evening, so we sat out on the terrace under a clear blue sky and had a few beers. The sun was still shining, glinting through the surrounding pine trees, and there was a gentle breeze off the lake, and the smell of pines. Chatter and laughter filled the air – especially at the next table, where a group of women in fancy dress were sitting.

Once we'd finished our beers and food, we walked back along the Saguenay River, crossing the Passerelle du Centenaire, an aluminium suspension bridge with two large triangular-shaped towers. I took a deep breath and filled my lungs with the beautiful smell of wild flowers floating up from the river bank. The real adventure was just starting, I thought to myself. Life doesn't get much better!

We turned in early to ensure ourselves a good night's sleep and to be ready for the next day's flying. I had a shower and hit the sack – once more tingling with excitement to get my hands on the fabulous machine again and wondering what amazing new sights, smells and sounds I would see in the morning.

4
TOWARDS THE BACK OF BEYOND

When we arrived at the airport early the next morning, the plan was to get three hours' flying under my belt and make it to Pourvoirie Mirage, the tiny fishing village that Mathieu had suggested. By this point, we would be far north and quite remote.

I'd plugged the coordinates into my SkyDemon navigation app to take us there, and lifted the craft smoothly into the air, enjoying the amazing power of the 505. We were off.

Soon it was just forest, stretching as far as the eye could see. On and on for endless miles I flew over this dark green carpet, without seeing any sign of civilisation. The further north we went, the more remote it became. I kept my eyes peeled for any tracks in the forest below, but even the logger tracks faded out after a while. It occurred to me that this would be a pretty awful place to suffer an engine failure. There were very few places where it might be possible to glide down to the ground without hitting a tree.

As we drew in closer to the pinpoint location, I started to have my doubts.

'Is this it?' I asked Martin.

'I can't see anyone,' he replied, peering forward.

I couldn't see anything that looked remotely like a place where you'd be able to refuel a helicopter – or even land one, for that matter. The ground below us was a carpet of fir trees, all a deep, dark green, occasionally broken by pockets of water.

As we approached one particularly rugged-looking rocky outcrop, however, we saw movement below. There were people out with some sort of machine – it looked like a roller – smoothing out the shingle.

'That must be it,' said Martin.

'I guess it must be.'

'Imagine living somewhere like this.'

'Rather you than me.'

I brought the helicopter down lower, took a look and decided this really must be it. I landed her to the side of the gravel track. On closer inspection, and with a bit of a shock, we realised this actually was the runway, but it didn't look very smooth. Runways in the UK are either tarmac or grass. This was just loose gravel. I would hate to have to land a plane on this surface and

I suspected they had to maintain it daily, smoothing it over continuously in order to keep it in a condition where planes could land. It really was unbelievable.

We were approached by an old man and a young lad.

The old man looked at us curiously. 'Where are you from?' he asked.

I explained that we had come from Alma and were flying to Europe. I think it was quite unusual to have a helicopter drop in unexpectedly on the tiny landing strip, especially during Covid.

'Can we refuel?' I asked.

The old man nodded and then the boy went over to a big generator and started tinkering around with it. After a few minutes, it was clear his efforts weren't having the intended result, so the old man went over to try to help him get the generator started.

My mind was racing. If they couldn't start the generator, we wouldn't be able to refuel. There was no 'plan B'; it was fuel or nothing. We couldn't go anywhere else, forwards or backwards.

After a nervous few minutes, the old boy did his magic and the generator coughed into life, rumbling unconvincingly, and then revved up. The kid gave us a thumbs-up, started pulling out the long hose and began pumping the fuel into the helicopter.

The next thing was to find fuel for ourselves. After three hours of flying, we were hungry.

'Is there anywhere to eat?' I asked.

'At the lodge,' said the old man, pointing ahead into the distance.

'How do we get there?'

'I'll take you.'

We climbed into a battered green pick-up truck, brushing the rubbish off the seats, and headed off down a bumpy dirt track. The lodge turned out to be a panelled one-storey building set against the trees and the edge of the lake. The view was stunning. It would have been wonderful to spend a night there and watch the sun set over the water.

We entered, unsure what to expect in those Covid days. We were greeted by an almost empty room with a manager and a chef seemingly trapped there, waiting for customers.

The manager approached and greeted us.

'Are you open for food?' I asked.

'Of course,' he replied with a smile, and led us to a table by the window.

'Looks like business must be hard,' I said, sitting down.

'Normally, this time of year, we would have 150 people in. This year, with Covid, we've had twelve visitors all season. It's a disaster.'

I felt sorry for the manager and his team. Covid had affected everyone, but seeing the impact on these small remote businesses which rely on people visiting them,

ARCTIC INSANITY

the true cost of the pandemic to individual livelihoods really hit me.

After soup, a salad and enormous plates of lasagne, we paid the bill and got up to leave. The manager kindly gave us a lift back to the airfield.

I pulled myself into the helicopter with a groaning stomach and mentally thanked Mathieu for knowing about this incredible place. We took off, heading into Inuit territory. The stops would only get more remote from here on.

5
A FROSTY WELCOME

From Pourvoirie Mirage it was just over three hours' flying to our next stop, Kuujjuaq. I loved these names, half of them French, half of them Inuit.

Until they were settled in villages by the government, the Inuit were migratory peoples who used land and marine resources to sustain themselves. They now live in small communities scattered across the Arctic and Subarctic. Many continue to practise a hunting-and-fishing lifestyle.

The French settlers in the 17th century referred to the Inuit as Eskimos. Today, they are described by their more local names, such as Yupik or Inupiat, or the more generic term Inuit.

After Pourvoirie Mirage, I was expecting Kuujjuaq to be a bustling metropolis. But in reality, only 2,750 people live in this isolated former Hudson's Bay Company trading post. In the 19th century, the

ARCTIC INSANITY

Beautiful Canadian scenery on the way to Kuujjuaq

village was a focus for trade between white settlers and the Inuit. Like many similar places in the region, it is still inhabited by small Inuit populations, their lightweight-looking little houses clustered along the snow-filled icy shores of the sea, with the mountains rising majestically behind.

Fortunately, Kuujjuaq has a good airport because of its position on the Koksoak River, near the estuary of the Hudson Strait. This was seen as strategically important by the Americans during the Second World War. The site on which they built their military base eventually became Kuujjuaq Airport. It is now a direct route to the remote areas of northern Canada, so the airport is well maintained by the government.

We approached Kuujjuaq pretty late in the day, when it was beginning to get dark. Seeing the airport lights on the horizon, I radioed the control tower and was guided into a spot alongside two Air Inuit planes. It was all easy, with no fuss. The airport only handles two flights a day, so the place was very quiet.

I asked the ground team if they could fill up the helicopter. They sprang into action immediately. When they were done, I asked one of them if he could recommend somewhere to eat. He offered to drive us into town. We jumped onto the back of a flat-bed pick-up truck and set off, with Martin and me standing on the back of the truck, gripping the roll bar as the wind blasted our faces.

We were dropped off at the Auberge Kuujjuaq Inn. Its exposed situation meant the flaking paint of its long timber-clad frontage was caked in a fresh layer of snow. All the vehicles parked in front of it were heavy-duty 4x4s – standard transport for this remote outpost – all covered in snow and ice.

Even in more normal times, I don't suppose Kuujjuaq residents are used to seeing outsiders. Since the Covid pandemic, they had presumably seen even fewer. When we walked up to reception at the Inn, the receptionist looked concerned. I'd pre-booked, so they were aware that we were on our way, but I'm not sure if he had received the memo.

'Have you guys just flown in?' he asked.

'Yeah. We've got a reservation for tonight,' I said.

He seemed hesitant. 'Where are you from?'

'I'm from England and Martin here is from Ireland.'

He pursed his lips. 'There's a problem, and the manager isn't here at the moment.'

He looked quite nervous. I suspected it was because of Covid.

'We've had our Covid tests, if that's what you're worried about.'

'I need to wait for my manager. I'm sure you can stay, but he wants to be here to check you in.'

We'd been flying for three and a half hours and been on the go for a very cold six hours, the sun had gone, the temperature was dropping and I wanted to sit down, chill out and soak up the atmosphere in the first Inuit town I had visited. I was absolutely gasping for a beer.

'Do you have a bar?' I asked.

'Yes,' he said. 'You have to go out the door, to the outside, and use the other entrance.'

'OK, we'll go and have a drink in the bar and wait for your manager there.'

We made our way back out into the snow and walked the twenty yards to the door. A burly man, dressed in dark, thick clothing, stopped us as we were about to walk through it.

'Where you guys from?' he asked.

'The UK,' I replied. 'We've flown in from Montreal.'

'You can't come in, lads,' he said, blocking the entrance.

Great, I thought. We'll sit out here and freeze to death then. I was starting to get a bit worried that we might have nowhere to sleep for the night. The helicopter cockpit didn't seem like the most enticing sleeping space in temperatures of minus 15C.

The door behind the bouncer opened and the receptionist poked his head out. 'These guys are OK,' he said. 'We're sorting out lodgings for them. You can let them have a drink.'

The bouncer nodded and let us pass into the warmth of the bar. We both had our bags with us and stuck out like sore thumbs. Everyone went silent, curious and possibly a little afraid to see two foreigners arrive in their isolated village during a global pandemic. To us, though, it was almost like walking into a cowboy saloon through the swinging doors, the honky-tonk piano cutting out and a hush falling over everyone.

I was tired and didn't care. I just wanted to sit down and have a beer.

We sat out of the way at the corner table, with its faded, worn leather seats, propping our bags up against the table. The waitress came over and we ordered a couple of pints and started planning our movements for the next couple of days, watched by some of the other customers.

About thirty minutes later, the receptionist turned up. From the expression on his face, I felt he was bearing bad news.

'They've said there's no way you can stay here,' he said.

'But I made a booking,' I said, beginning to get annoyed.

'You've got to stay somewhere else.'

'Where?' With Covid, I feared a lot of places would have shut their doors.

'There's the Charlie Kudluk Cooperative. I can give them a call and see if they'll let you in.'

To our ears this sounded a strange name for a hotel, but at this point all we wanted was a warm place to get our heads down for a few hours.

'That would be great.' I tried my best to smile, as if we were grateful for the favour he was doing us.

'Don't rush,' he said. 'Finish your beers.'

I thought it strange that they were happy to have us in the bar but that we couldn't stay, but maybe it was best not to say so. They might change their minds about letting us in the bar.

I beckoned to the waitress for two more beers.

'Do you have anything to eat?' Martin asked.

'I'll ask the kitchen.'

It turned out they had four slices of pizza left in the

whole place – and that was our dinner. I had never imagined that food might be a major problem in Canada, but it was turning out to be one of the more difficult resources to obtain.

The receptionist came back to say he had managed to get us a reservation. Once we had finished our slices of pizza and the last dregs of the beer, we paid up, grabbed our bags and walked around the corner to the Charlie Kudluk Cooperative.

The Cooperative was a forgettable building: simple, functional but, hopefully, warm. We walked into reception and the guy behind the desk seemed to be waiting for us. He led us down a corridor and opened a door at the end of it, explaining that we had the use of a communal toilet, shower and kitchen.

'We've got cameras on all the kitchens,' he said.

I nodded.

'If you leave any mess or don't wash up after yourselves it's a fine of a hundred Canadian dollars.'

Not a warm welcome, but still, it was a bed for the night. We weren't planning on using the kitchen; this was just a place to get our heads down.

I woke next morning feeling shattered, and could barely pull myself out of bed. I realised that when flying in these remote harsh areas, with little chance of rescue, the adrenaline runs high all day – and then you get the comedown. I was desperate for a nice cup of tea to wake me up. I headed to the kitchen with the receptionist's words ringing in my ears. I found some Weetabix and a teabag and made a quick brew, then looked up at the camera and made sure I washed my bowl, cup and spoon, dried them and put them back in the cupboard.

Now I was all set for the onward journey into the rock and ice of the remote northern regions of Canada – provided someone would give us a lift back to the airport.

6
POOR VISIBILITY

Fortunately, getting out of Kuujjuaq proved a lot easier than finding a place willing to let us stay the night. One phone call from the reception of the Cooperative, and a big 4x4 truck turned up to take us back to the airstrip.

Flight check complete and the blades revving up over my head, I was pleased to be back in the air again. From Kuujjuaq we aimed to fly to Iqaluit, Canada's most northern city, formerly known as Frobisher Bay. The capital of the Nunavut territory, it's on Baffin Island. This would be our first time flying over water – freezing water – so I'd double-checked everything was good before take-off.

As the flight time was five hours, this would also be the first time we'd be using the full tank of fuel and trialling the make-shift reserve tank. To say I had my fingers crossed would be a significant understatement.

Baffin Island is separated from the mainland by the

Hudson Strait, some 200 miles across, which joins the vast Hudson Bay to the Atlantic Ocean. When we set off from Kuujjuaq, I flew virtually straight out across the waters of Ungava Bay. We could have taken a longer route and crawled up the coast for a while, but this was a long leg and we decided to fly straight across the water to conserve fuel and keep the route time as short as possible in case the weather closed in.

As I shot out over the water, a thought occurred to me. 'Martin, we've forgotten something.'

'What?'

'We're out over the freezing water but we forgot to put our dry suits on.'

'Shit!'

That was putting it mildly.

A dry suit is designed to protect you when flying over stretches of icy water, should the worst happen and you end up in the sea. The water in this part of the world is full of icebergs and so cold that if you went in, you would only have a couple of minutes before your organs started shutting down. With luck, the dry suit would help extend that time to several hours if worn correctly and zipped up tightly (which is not comfortable). Hopefully, enough time for you to get your life raft out.

We didn't have enough fuel to turn around and put our suits on, so it was a matter of just praying and hoping. I tried to put the problem to the back of my mind as I looked at the view. I could see coast to coast and it was truly stunning. The Hudson Strait seemed to stretch for miles to the east and west. The early morning sun made the water look serene and calm. I knew it wouldn't seem so inviting if our reserve tank conked out, plunging us head first into it, but I was determined to enjoy our ride, despite our schoolboy error over the dry suits.

Slightly to our east was Akpatok Island, at the entrance to the bay. The island is flanked by enormous, sheer, white limestone cliffs that rise up to 800ft above sea level. They looked absolutely spectacular. I made a mental note to try and return to explore this beautiful, inaccessible place one day.

Our route took us right along the edge of the Akpatok cliffs. This was one of those moments that made everything feel worthwhile. At times, the logistics involved in arranging this trip had made me question whether it was really worth putting myself through all this for the sake of saving a few quid for somebody else. But as we zipped over the glistening water, with the white cliffs to our right and the sun shining gently above them, I reflected that this was exactly what this adventure was all about – why I was there. The moments with views like these are the moments pilots dream of.

My deep sense of completeness and satisfaction didn't last long, however.

We cleared the island and were making our way out into the Hudson Strait proper, when ominous black clouds and fog started forming. Fog is a helicopter pilot's worst nightmare, and this weather came down almost out of nowhere. Visibility dropped a staggering amount in a matter of seconds. It was as if someone had suddenly thrown a giant grey blanket over the windows.

'Bugger,' I said. 'This isn't good.'

We might have tried flying under the cloud but if it descended any further and enveloped us we'd be dead. In a helicopter you're hanging like a bauble from the blades and once in the clouds it's very difficult to work out which way is up, so it's very easy to turn the machine over. For those who ski, it's a bit like being on the slopes covered in cloud, unable to work out whether your skis are moving forward – except in a helicopter, it's three-dimensional and the feeling is far worse.

I glanced across to the west. In the distance I could make out some lights through the cloud. I looked at my SkyDemon map.

'It's Quaqtaq,' I said to Martin.'

'You sure?' he said.'

'I think so.'

Quaqtaq was another Inuit village at the northwestern tip of Umava Bay, where the large inlet meets the Hudson Strait. I'd scoped the place out while prepping our route. It was slightly off course, so I didn't end up including it, but now it might prove to be a lifeline.

The fog was eating up the sea behind us as we continued to fly north; ahead of us, the outlook was seriously bleak. The icy sea stretched out beneath us and, of course, neither of us was wearing a dry suit. So much for putting that problem out of our minds. Contemplating the freezing cold sea, I knew that we'd die within minutes if submerged in it.

I re-adjusted my course and started making my way towards Quaqtaq, reasoning that it would be better to land, refuel, wait for the weather to pass and then head out again. It would put us even further behind schedule, but it seemed the sensible course of action.

Ten minutes later, Martin started fidgeting.

'I think we can do this,' he said.

'Do what?' I asked, knowing exactly what he meant.

'I think we can cross the strait.'

'You reckon?'

'Let's give it a shot.'

Bloody hell, give it a shot? This was the first big water stretch we'd done; it's a long distance over the Hudson Strait – probably 100 miles or so – and a) we couldn't see a bloody thing while b) not wearing dry suits, but we were 'giving it a shot'.

'Sure,' I said.

If you're going to agree to something that you know

is a stupid idea, at least give it some male bravado and sound like you're convinced.

Actually, my only reason for agreeing was that I figured I could turn back at any moment, provided the fog didn't close in behind us.

So we headed out into the murky, horrible, rainy weather. I'd been very lucky with flying conditions until this point, but now here I was, facing some of the worst imaginable weather at the worst imaginable moment. It was the first time I was really putting the helicopter – and ourselves – to the test.

We ploughed on for what felt like an eternity. The view outside was of rain streaming down the windscreen, making it very hard to see into the murk; the only reference point was the sea, a very short distance below. I started seeing phantom shapes, imagining darker shadows indicating land where there was none. Instead I tried to focus on the instruments, making sure I kept our speed and direction consistent. We'd see land eventually, I hoped.

Around an hour or so later, one of the dark smudges through the windscreen morphed into something representing the gentle gradient of land. I stared very hard at the shape through the rain-covered windscreen, praying I was right. As we got closer, I realised it really was land. I'd never been so glad to see solid ground. At least now if the weather closed in, we had a fighting chance of being able to put the helicopter down.

As we left the murky, rain-drenched strait behind, the weather front began to clear and I could make out the trees below. Iqaluit was close to the sea, so I made my way straight towards Iqaluit airport. All I could think about was being able to set down on *terra firma*.

I could sense Martin buzzing about the prospect of landing at Iqaluit. The settlement is the largest community in the eastern Canadian Arctic, established as a trading post in 1914 and becoming an airbase during the Second World War. Later, it was the site of construction camps for a line of Cold War radar stations, which meant the airbase grew in significance, and landing there became a source of pride to any pilot who did so. It continues to hold legendary status among the flying community.

We landed next to the two-storey Frobisher Bay Touchdown Services building. Giant red letters on the roof said FBO, standing for Fixed Base Operator. It's the term given to commercial enterprises that have been granted the right by an airport authority to provide aviation services, such as fuelling, aircraft maintenance, parking, food and so on. It had been built during the Second World War and was still serving private aircraft.

First, though, the usual fuss about refuelling. I wanted to fuel up straight away, as I'd really stretched our supplies to their limit, especially with the slight diversion I'd taken towards Quaqtaq before we changed our minds and decided to crack on. We'd basically done two legs of a triangle, flying for about four and a half hours (with five our upper limit).

The guy with the fuel truck turned up and started prepping to refuel.

'Could you also fill up our reserve tank?' I requested.

I showed him the fuel sack where the back seats used to be, deflated after we'd used up the fuel on the crossing.

He sucked his teeth. 'I can't fuel that up.'

'You can.' I tried not to let my irritation show. 'We filled it up in Kuujjuaq. No problem at all.'

He looked unsure. 'You did?'

'It's integrated. It's part of the design for our trip.'

This back-and-forth went on for another ten minutes or so before he eventually gave in and agreed to fuel up both tanks. Without both tanks we couldn't proceed with the trip.

I thanked him and we made our way inside the FBO to pay. I slumped into a large leather sofa in the lounge, where a globe hung from the ceiling and the pelt of a polar bear was attached to a wall. I was exhausted. Still excited to be in Iqaluit, Martin seemed fascinated by the building.

After five minutes I went back outside to see how the fuelling was going. I noticed with horror that there was oil on the tail of the helicopter. The aircraft is white, so oil really shows up, and there was definitely some on the tail fin. This meant something was leaking. I was concerned it might be hydraulic fluid. The two main controls – cyclic and collective – are run on hydraulic fluid systems called servos, like the power steering on a car. Without this, it's very hard to control the craft. I have done a landing without this 'power steering', but I found it very tough, and I'm six-foot-three, so I'm no weakling. I didn't want to do another one, and particularly not in an emergency situation on the ice.

I got down on my knees and peered under the engine. I could see oil under one of the hydraulic lines. It definitely looked as though the line was leaking. We could not fly like this. The whole trip was at risk and we and the helicopter could end up stranded at one of the world's most isolated airports.

I went back into the FBO building and asked the receptionist if there were any aircraft mechanics/engineers around. Even better, helicopter engineers. To my intense relief, he told me there were some mechanics, although there was only one helicopter maintenance company in the airport.

Well, that was a start. He gave me the company's number. I rang with bated breath. A man answered, saying they only had one guy on that day, but if I went to their large hangar he might be in there. What if he wasn't? Still, this was my only chance.

I wandered out into the freezing cold and took the ten-minute walk across the airport's icy tarmac to the large hangar. Inside was a massive Sikorsky S-92 helicopter that can carry up to 20 people – a magnificent beast. But I couldn't see a soul.

'Hello, anybody here?'

No answer. I shouted louder. Again, no answer.

Then a man's head appeared from under another helicopter. 'Hi, can I help?'

I explained that I had a hydraulic leak in my helicopter, that I was on my way to Europe, and begged him to take a look, saying I would be more than happy to compensate him generously for his time.

The whole trip hinged on this man.

'Let me grab my tools and ladder,' he said.

Although all helicopter maintenance engineers are trained on specific helicopter types, he told me he wasn't trained on the Bell 505. Nevertheless, I prayed he would be able to help.

He invited me to get into his truck, and we sped to the helicopter. I showed him the join where I thought the leak was. He climbed up his ladder and looked at the pipe work, studying it carefully. Then he got his spanners out and tried to tighten the joint; nothing. He tried again; nothing.

'It's really stiff,' he said, cursing under his breath. 'I'll see if I can loosen it and re-tighten it.'

But it wouldn't move. He said in his view there was nothing wrong with that coupling, so the leak must be coming from somewhere else. Shit. What now? The joint was definitely dripping oil, but I understood his point. It could just as easily be coming from somewhere else and running down the pipe to drip at the joint.

I thanked him for his help and asked how much I owed him.

'Nothing,' he replied.

What a fantastic bloke, I thought. It had been so long since anybody had done me a favour for nothing that I had forgotten what it felt like. Perhaps in these desolate parts people are still more generous with their time – I guess in such freezing, remote areas you never know when you're going to need a favour back from someone.

I headed back into the FBO, where I called Bell to explain the problem.

'It may be engine oil,' said a mechanic. 'How full is she?'

'She's just below the full line but above the minimum.'

'Just top her right up and you should be OK.'

What if it wasn't OK? There seemed to be a lot of 'shoulds' on this trip and I felt like a cat with nine lives that were fast running out. If we ran short on oil, the engine would seize and we would drop out of the sky. However, I had no choice but to trust Bell and give it a go.

That'll be on my gravestone: 'He gave it a go!'

I climbed onto the helicopter roof with the spare can

of engine oil that Bell had given me in Mirabel and poured it in, right up to the max line. We were now full to the brim. I just had to remember to check the oil regularly and hope to hell there would be somewhere to land to make the check on the next leg.

I hurried back into the FBO to get Martin.

'Nice little aircraft you've got here,' said a man in torn blue overalls.

'Thanks.'

'Where you headed?'

'Final stop is Europe – Guernsey,' I said. 'But today we're off to Pangnirtung.'

It always raised an eyebrow among people at our stops when they heard we were going all the way to Europe. Some were fascinated; others sceptical. This guy was firmly in the latter camp. And he also seemed more concerned with our more immediate destination.

'Good luck in Pangnirtung,' he said.

'What do you mean?'

'They ain't letting anyone into town. Covid and all that.'

'We've had tests and we've got negative results.'

'Don't think that'll matter much to them. You'll see.'

'We don't have any choice,' I said. 'So I guess we will.'

Welcome to Canada, I thought. This guy was clearly Mr Pessimist. I was tired. It had been a stressful stop and I didn't want any more negative vibes. I just wanted to get in the air and crack on. We'd deal with whatever Pangnirtung might throw at us when we got there.

We were very aware of the Covid pandemic and the concern people could feel when two random men landed in their town. We were taking all the necessary precautions: gloves and masks whenever we were outside the helicopter. We had all the permissions necessary from the authorities. Plus, we'd had Covid tests prior to setting off, so we were confident we weren't a risk to anyone else.

'You won't get accommodation in Pangnirtung,' Mr Pessimist added, jumping into his truck and driving off without another word.

I clambered into the cockpit. Another two hours to Pangnirtung, our last port of call in Canada before we attempted the incredibly dangerous ocean crossing to Greenland.

We'd soon find out whether the place was as inhospitable as Mr Pessimist claimed.

7
INTO THE WHITE

The flight from Iqaluit made us appreciate how remote we were in the far north of Canada. Iqaluit was the only real point of civilisation on Baffin Island. The rest was freezing desolate rock, a snow-scarred and bleak landscape, with icy rivers and lakes peppering the ground below us as we whizzed overhead. Even the trees struggled to survive. There were only a few small conifers dotted near water sources now.

On the flight, we saw no human structures, no roads, no buildings; nothing. It was humbling to be out here, to see this almost untouched wilderness, zipping away 500ft below us. In fact, it was scary, but totally exhilarating at the same time. That massive island, twice the size of the UK, and it was just us, completely free to fly where we wanted.

After an hour and a half of flying, we were about thirty minutes from Pangnirtung. I radioed up to them, giving them giving the call sign of our helicopter and saying we were inbound, approaching from the southwest.

The radio crackled but returned only silence.

I repeated my message, adding: 'Request radio check and weather report.'

Nothing. For goodness' sake.

'Hey, Martin, can you grab the controls?'

I pulled my mobile out and punched in the airport's telephone number manually. The call rang and rang, eventually dialling out.

'What do we do?' said Martin.

'Not much we can do. We can't just keep flying around in circles. I'll free call and take her in.'

Martin didn't demur.

I made several open calls to warn any other aircraft in the vicinity of our presence, and then approached the very small, rudimentary gravel landing strip next to a yellow building that looked more like a school than a terminal building. It was right in the middle of the village, which was a small rambling collection of tin-roofed huts. When I say 'in the middle of the village', I'm honestly not exaggerating: the nearest hut was a mere 50 metres from the gravel runway. Their windows must rattle like hell when planes come in. But what I hadn't appreciated yet was that few planes do come in. The airfield was really an emergency medical evacuation route.

I saw a good spot to land, away from the runway, just in case an emergency plane needed to come in. I hovered, glancing towards the tower, which was completely devoid of life. With one last shrug at Martin, I brought the helicopter in and touched down on the gravel.

I jumped out of the aircraft, expecting to see some form of movement sparked by our arrival. The freezing cold wind lashed my face, in stark contrast with the relative warmth of the cockpit. I shivered.

'What now?' said Martin, who had joined me on the gravel, as we set out to walk towards the terminal building.

'Your guess is as good as mine. We're really in the back end of beyond now.'

Just as we were beginning to think the whole place was totally deserted, a door in the terminal building opened and a stocky Inuit man emerged. He raised a gloved hand over his head in greeting and beckoned us over to him.

As we drew closer, he eyed us suspiciously, standing in the open doorway like a bouncer. By now, we were wearing our surgical masks and gloves, and we stopped short of him so as not to encroach on his space.

'Sorry for dropping in unannounced; we couldn't get anybody on the radio,' I said.

'There has not been much need to operate the tower recently,' he said.

INTO THE WHITE

On the way to Pangnirtung – before the weather turned

'We need to refuel, and we have accommodation booked for the night.'

Of course, he wanted to know where we had come from. I told him.

'We are worried about the pandemic here,' he said.

'That's understandable. But we've have had tests. Both of us are negative.'

He seemed to visibly loosen up once he heard that, but there was a long pause before he spoke again.

'We can refuel you,' he said at last. 'You'll need to pay at the Co-op.'

'Sorry? The Co-op?' I couldn't believe it. Out here in the middle of bloody nowhere there was a Co-op!

'The supermarket in town. It's the big yellow

building to the north, past the post office.'

'What about the Auyuittuq Lodge?' This was the hostel where we had reserved rooms.

He pointed ahead. 'It's that red building by the water.'

He handed me a chit, which I assumed must be marked with the fuel we needed. 'Give them this at the Co-op and pay.'

I returned to the helicopter to tie down the blades, as the weather was windy and horribly cold. We then made our way back towards the terminal building and out through a gate in the fence. We now saw that the village of Pangnirtung had been deliberately built with the runway at its centre, since this was the only means for the inhabitants to receive medical treatment and emergency supplies to help them survive in the brutal winters. It was weird. We were standing right in the middle of the village.

The ground was covered in thick snow and ice. We trudged towards the houses. I noticed a lot of them had discarded furniture outside. This one a broken table, that one an old sofa; each left to rot in the layers of snow that had built up on top of them. The place seemed like a ghetto.

Battered four-wheel-drive trucks passed us as we made our way into the village. The occupants, huddled under layers of warm clothing, stared out of their half-fogged-up windows at us. We must have been a sight:

two six-foot-plus Westerners dressed in bright-orange pilot survival gear in a village where the average height was around five foot four. With the Covid pandemic, they probably hadn't seen any outsiders for months.

In the distance, I could see the road sloping down to the harbour. The village was built on a small plateau with an estuary on one side and a sharp cliff face of apocalyptic proportions on the other. From our position we had a spectacular view up the estuary. It looked very bleak, icy and cold, but very beautiful in its own way.

Down by the waterfront were dozens of little fishing boats, each a bright speck of colour against the greys, whites and blacks of the rocky, snow-filled landscape. The harbour itself was quite modern as, much like the airport, it was another vital lifeline for the Inuit people who lived here.

We went first to the Auyuittuq Lodge. It was a wooden shack with a corrugated tin roof, three storeys high. The red paint was flaking. We had a reservation, but there was no one around, so we just dropped our gear and I headed out to the Co-op to pay for the fuel. To me, it was more like a corner shop than a supermarket, and it was stacked with all manner of food and snacks, including Coca-Cola and Pot Noodles. Unsurprisingly, it was lacking in anything fresh. Behind the counter was an Inuit girl with her head stuck in a magazine.

I put down the fuel chit I'd been given. 'I'd like to pay

for some jet fuel please,' I said, feeling very conscious of how ridiculous it sounded to be saying this in such a small food shop in the middle of nowhere.

The girl put down her magazine, seeming unfazed. She swiped the chit off the counter.

'You come in the bird?' she asked.

I smiled. 'That's correct.'

'Where you go?'

'Europe. To Guernsey.'

'Take me with you?'

I saw a glint in her eyes. I wasn't sure if she was joking or not. I felt she really might gladly jump at the chance to fill Martin's seat if I were to kick him out – regardless of the danger, or of the fact that she had likely never been out of her small village.

'You really want to go?'

'Yes. Take me to Europeland.'

'As much as I would love to, there are only two seats. Besides, if I took you there, how would you get back?'

'I don't care.' She really did seem to be serious.

As I left the Co-op, I reflected on that conversation. She was clearly desperate to get away from Pangnirtung. From what I'd heard, the people who lived in these villages were paid peanuts. They had enough money to exist, but never enough to leave to explore our beautiful world. I felt for her.

Still thinking about how trapped she must feel, I made my way to the Auyuittuq Lodge, where I'd left

Martin. It turned out that the lodge was run by a non-Inuit Canadian woman, and was only open for six months of the year.

Telling us dinner was ready in the lounge, she led us upstairs to the first floor and into a large room with three tables and chairs and a couple of old sofas positioned in front of an ancient TV. It all looked like a 1970s school common room, but we didn't need luxury; these serviceable buildings were like oases in a freezing-cold, desolate landscape. Through the big window I could see out across the cold white estuary and the high snow-covered cliffs on the other side. It was unbelievable, like something out of a sales brochure.

For a moment I was completely lost to everything beyond drinking in such beautiful scenery. Then, I came back to my senses and wondered what might be for dinner.

It turned out to be two huge plates filled with steak, peas and potatoes, all smothered in gravy. It was proper man-grub. Both Martin and I dived in, making short work of the food. It was amazing how much hunger built up when I was putting in seven hours or so of flying during the day. They say mental exercise is as exhausting as physical, and it was certainly hard work concentrating up in that bird all day in these conditions. I didn't really get a chance to stop; my hands and feet were always working to make sure I kept the craft in the air. All I could do was grab a few sweeties from time to time to stave off the worst of the hunger. That meant that any time I had the chance to tuck into some good food like this, I relished it.

The plan for the next day was to get up at 3am, leaving plenty of time for the big crossing to Greenland. I didn't even unpack my bag. We were aiming to make the crossing as soon as there was light to see by.

I didn't know whether I would get any sleep that night, or what dangers the morning would hold. This was going to be the toughest test of the trip for Martin and me, and for the helicopter.

8
ABORTED MISSION

My alarm beeped at three. I rolled out of bed, stumbled to the shower and blasted cold water on my face to bring me to my senses. I am wide awake at night but terrible in the mornings. I think I was made for clubbing.

Much more alert after the shower and splash of cold water, I went back to my room and opened the curtains. For a second, I thought someone was pulling some sort of joke and had draped a carpet over my window, because I couldn't see a thing. Then shock set in as I realised I was looking out at extremely close fog. On top of that, there was rain pounding against the pane. Everything was grey and horrible: absolutely terrible flying weather.

I met Martin in the common room. He was sitting at one of the long tables studying a map.

'Not great out,' I said.

'You can say that again,' he grimaced.

'What do you think?'

He looked up from the map.

'I don't know. What do you reckon?'

I stood next to the table, watching the rain lashing the windows as I pulled up the satellite image on my phone. 'Hmmm. If we could just clear these cliffs behind us... Let's give it a shot; see what happens. We're already behind schedule.'

That was enough for Martin. He folded up the map, packed it back into his pocket and stood up.

'Alright,' he said. 'Let's give it a go.'

I pulled the front door of the lodge shut on the latch and posted the room keys through the letter box. We then made our way out into the cold. The fog had made the temperature noticeably lower than it had been the previous day, at minus 10°C. We hunched against the wind and rain as we made our way up the short hill to the landing strip.

In theory, we could fly the helicopter with visibility this low: we were both trained to do so, as it's a mandatory part of learning. I'd used foggles during my lessons – special glasses that simulate fog conditions so you're flying off the instruments only. But we were advised never to do it except in extreme emergencies. And the difference between foggles and the real thing is that you can simply take off the foggles if things go wrong, and look outside and there won't be many unexpected mountains or fjords. This, on the other hand, was the real deal. The stakes were very high; we couldn't afford to make any mistakes.

The helicopter was ready and refuelled by the side of the runway. I checked the oil again, ran through the external pre-flight check list and removed the blade tie-down before jumping into the cockpit and firing her up. Exchanging a nervous glance with Martin, I pulled back on the cyclic and we lifted into the torrential rain and fog.

We shot upwards – necessary in order to clear the massive cliff face next to Pangnirtung. Up and up we went, glimpsing occasional patches of cliff through the fog and rain. Going over the cliffs was the shortest route, shorter than going around along the coast, and fuel conservation was an absolute must on this leg – four hours 35 minutes flying on a five-hour tank, giving us only 25 minutes of contingency. I was hoping – praying, really – that the fog was low-lying and we'd be able to get above it and see where we were going.

However, as we continued upwards the visibility seemed if anything to be decreasing.

Then something moved in the fog and a dark shape rushed towards us.

I pulled back harder on the cyclic, clenching my teeth at the strain. The nose of the helicopter rose… and the top of the cliff face passed silently underneath us. Far too close for comfort.

'Shit!' I said under my breath.

Martin looked calm, but I noticed he was gripping his seat intensely, his knuckles white.

Rain was pouring down the windscreen and there weren't any wipers.

'I can't see a bloody thing, mate,' I said.

We had the internal blowers on the windscreen, trying to clear it, but with the rain bashing into us it was next to impossible. It was like driving a car down the motorway at high speed with no wiper blades. All I could see was a blur, like looking through dishwater, and I could barely make anything out.

I saw on the map that we were on top of the peninsula and would shortly cross into the next fjord. If I could just navigate over this bit of terrain I should be able to drop down into the fjord and below the fog.

We skated along the plateau, dodging the clouds and looking for a small gap. After what seemed like ages I found one, and we shot through, cleared the plateau and dropped down into the next fjord, relying heavily on the aircraft instruments rather than any information coming from outside. I turned left to fly along the fjord, knowing that at the end of it we would have to rise steeply again to get over the next cliff face and out over the open sea.

'What do you want to do?' I asked Martin.

'I don't know,' he said. 'You're the captain.'

'This is madness. I can't see a bloody thing through

this torrential rain. I think we should go back.'

'OK, let's do it.'

No debate.

Rather than risking going back over the fjord cliffs, I opted for the long route along the sea, around the edge of the fjord and then making my way back up to Pangnirtung. Rain continuously lashed against the windscreen and I struggled all the way back to see where I was going. After what seemed like an eternity, but was actually only an hour and three quarters, I glimpsed the houses and the yellow control tower through the fog. Boy, was I glad to see that again. I landed back at the same spot that we had left just under two hours earlier.

I felt truly knackered and my nerves were totally frayed from two hours of intense concentration and not knowing if we were going to make it out, or back. I was just happy to be back on solid ground. The only issue was that our flight had used up some of the fuel we needed to make the crossing to Greenland, so we would need to refuel again.

We had surely made the right decision to turn back. Despite my deep disappointment about not being able to push on, I had lived to tell the tale another day. As someone once said, 'There are old pilots and bold pilots, but there are no old, bold pilots.'

We had arrived back in Pangnirtung at 6am and the village was silent. We trudged back to Auyuittuq

Lodge, following our own undisturbed footprints in the snow. Already we were deflated to be losing another day, but when we reached the lodge we were faced with a new problem.

I walked up to the hotel porch and pushed the door. It was locked fast – and we had of course posted the keys through the letter box earlier that morning. Damn! I tried gently prising the front door, hoping the pressure would open it; nothing.

It was now 6.30am and the temperature was minus 5°C. We'd had extremely little sleep and the door to the lodge was firmly locked. If we didn't find shelter soon, we'd freeze to death. I could see the headlines: 'Two helicopter pilots survive terrifying helicopter ordeal... only to die from exposure because they couldn't get back into their hotel!'

Because it was so early, we had initially been cautious about making too much noise, but now I was no longer bothered about disturbing anyone's sleep; our survival depended on waking them up. I started banging very loudly on the door. When that had no effect, I shouted through the letter box. But still nobody stirred.

Our last hope was a notice on the door with a number to call for guests arriving out of hours. I pulled my glove off with my teeth and grabbed my phone, punching in the numbers with numb fingers as my breath fogged the screen.

By now, I hadn't really expected anyone to answer,

but my heart still sank when the call rang off.

'What do we do?' asked Martin.

'Don't know,' I replied, anxiously looking around me.

'I mean, Christ, we can't stand here all morning. It doesn't open until ten.'

I blew my cheeks out. 'Yeah, we've got to find a way in somehow or we'll freeze to death.'

9
CALLING THE POLICE

I surveyed the building, looking for some way to get inside. There was a window on the second floor that looked like it might be open.

'Right,' I said. 'I'm going to climb up onto the roof and aim for that window. Hopefully I'll be able to get in and then let you in.'

Martin looked sceptical. The window was pretty high up, and everything was freezing cold, icy and slippery. Whereas I was thinking, I have climbed Everest, so I am blooming sure I can climb up to the second floor of a building.

There was a single-storey outbuilding on the side of the lodge. I grabbed a table that had been dumped outside the house next door to give me enough height to reach the first-floor roof. Even at six-foot-three, with the added height of the table, I had to reach high to grab the roof. My hands – lumps of ice at this point

– struggled to grasp the corrugated tin and I slipped. Over went the table, and I landed face down in the snow. Bugger. I picked myself and the table up.

On the second attempt, I somehow managed to get a loose hand grip on the slippery roof and haul my body up onto it. I prayed the tin would hold my weight – 15 stone of English beef.

I crawled along the edge, where I hoped the roof was strongest, slowly making my way around to an exposed drainpipe. The roof creaked ominously under my weight.

I grabbed the drainpipe and used it to shimmy up to the second-floor flat roof. So far, so good. I hadn't gone through the roof, and no criminal damage or broken bones.

On the second-floor roof there was a glass conservatory with small windows. Looking through one of them, I saw what seemed to be some sort of meeting room.

I found one window slightly open and stuck my fingers into the tiny gap, trying to push the window catch up to free the window. It was fiendishly difficult and I couldn't quite reach. I took off my glove – my hand was freezing, as I had now been at this caper for 45 minutes. I pulled up my sleeve and gently eased my hand through the gap. I could just touch the bar. I flicked it with my fingertip – and finally pushed it up. I could then pull the window open towards me. There was about a 10-inch gap.

Bloody hell! I wasn't even sure my head would fit through that. The windows were low down, so I had to lie on the flat roof covered in snow, then try to poke my head under the window and upwards. At least my head fitted. So far so good.

Next, I needed to remove my jacket and jumper to make myself as slim as possible before trying to squeeze through. I thought of throwing my jumper and jacket in through the window first but stopped in the nick of time. If I couldn't get through, with no jumper or jacket I'd freeze to death in about half an hour.

I eased my head through the opening, rejoicing as a warm blast of air met me from the room. I squeezed my shoulders together, squirming from side to side like a snake, and very slowly they inched their way through the opening. My chest was now suspended on the window latch – not comfortable. It was a good three-foot drop down to the floor and I couldn't get any leverage to help me drag the rest of my body through the window.

I reached out with my hand and managed to grab the back of a chair positioned around the conference table. I dragged it towards me, placing it directly under the window. Grabbing its back with both hands, I then pushed upwards from it to try to pull the rest of my body through the window. Hauling my hips through required endless wriggling backwards and forwards.

When they finally eased through, my testicles ended up positioned directly over the window catch. I don't recommend you try this at home.

Suddenly I felt my hands slipping off the chair, and things happened quickly. I shot forwards, praying my feet would get stuck, but they too burst through the window at high speed and I ended up on the floor in a heap. I uncoiled cautiously. There would be sizeable bruises on my ankle, knee and left elbow, but thankfully my testicles were in place and I seemed to be otherwise OK.

I'd done it! I now hoped fervently that the conference room door wasn't locked – because there was no way I was going back out through that window…

It opened.

It had taken the best part of an hour but I was back in the lodge. I walked down to the front door and opened the latch.

Martin was shivering outside. 'Well done, mate,' he said, as he shot through the door into the warmth.

Our old rooms were locked so we walked up the stairs to the first-floor lounge with its big old dining table, sticky old leather sofas and its spectacular picture window. Without another word, I lay down on the nearest sofa and was asleep within minutes. Flying all day is hard work, but I had never anticipated how tiring it would be to wake up early then break into a hotel in a freezing climate.

When I woke up several hours later, the owner of the lodge was looking down at me with a concerned expression. I explained the situation to her and apologised for having had to resort to breaking in. She didn't seem to mind all that much, and was more than happy for us to stay another night.

The problem was, we were stuck in Pangnirtung for the day. We couldn't go anywhere – there was nothing to do and nowhere to go in the village, meaning that the day was a write-off. Even if the weather improved around lunchtime, the time frame would be too tight for us to get over to Greenland with enough time to react if something went wrong or we needed to make some sort of detour.

So we just wrote the day off, and sat there all day, checking the weather, chatting and playing cards. I was absolutely shattered from the mental and physical work of the day up to that point, so it was good to rest, but I couldn't resist continually checking the weather.

At least this enabled me also to go on making the most of that stunning view, stretching away far up the fjord. It continued to mesmerise me. I watched the fog rise, sink, rise, sink, rise, sink. On all sides, steep mountains rose up about 500 feet from the little sandy plateau in the middle of nowhere on which Pangnirtung sits.

It was actually the Hudson's Bay Trading Company that founded the trading post here at Pangnirtung, in the early 1920s. The plateau was very flat, and big enough, it turned out, to fit a runway. What was truly remarkable, though, was that the Inuit and their predecessors had found ways to survive and thrive in this area for millennia before the Hudson's Bay Company and the whaling business arrived.

Having nearly frozen on the roof of the lodge that morning, I understood more fully why they'd decided to stick the airport right in the centre of town. We'd arrived in the middle of summer and I could still easily have died of cold. I couldn't imagine even the locals would be particularly keen on spending long periods outside during the winter, when the snow must lie many metres deep. So you certainly wouldn't want to be walking a long way from the plane to wherever you were going.

In the other direction, away from the mountain, were two huge industrial silos – incredibly ugly things, stuck on the edge of town. One was for aircraft fuel, because the aircraft were the locals' lifeline; and the other was for domestic heating fuel. Each was vital for survival out here.

As I contemplated the containers, I noticed a huge ship quite far out off the coast.

'What's that ship doing?' I asked the woman who ran the hotel.

She looked over.

'It's the oil ship,' she said.

'But it's a quarter of a kilometre out to sea.'

'It can't get any closer.'

'How does it get the oil into the tanks?'

'By pipe. Look at that guy unrolling it.'

Sure enough, I could see a guy in a little boat, somewhere between the ship and the land. He seemed to be rolling out some sort of cable, a sort of flexible pipe that floated on the ocean, snaking to the shore from the ship.

'How often do they come and do that?'

'Twice a year.'

I felt very privileged to be there on the day they pumped the fuel in. It was quite extraordinary to see how remote settlements like this survived in their harsh environment. I wondered how on earth they had managed in the old days. They must have used whale and seal blubber as a means of heating, but it would have been much tougher to hunt and gather to meet their needs than having fuel shipped over for you.

The Inuit are remarkable people. They would have been wearing the skins of the animal and using its blubber for heat, they would have cooked with the oils and eaten the meat for sustenance. Everything had a purpose; everything was a tool for survival.

Obviously, they have modernised with their big fuel tanks, but now they seem to be totally dependent on them. If the fjord froze up completely and the ship was unable to get close enough to pump the fuel, what then? Would enough of them still have the hunting knowledge they need to make it through the coldest seasons? I hoped they did.

Thinking about how the Inuit survived made me remember that we needed to pick up some supplies for the rest of the trip, so we left the lodge and made our way to the supermarket. It was all about survival, if anything went wrong with the helicopter. If we had a problem, and I was forced to land far from any airport, we had a tent in which we could survive for several days; we just needed to top up the food supplies to make sure we were covered.

We needed a lot, too. In that sort of environment, our bodies would burn off a vast number of calories. I remembered that for Everest, both times, I was told the body burned off the equivalent of twenty-four Christmas dinners to get to the summit. It's basically working really hard to generate enough heat to keep you alive.

If we crash-landed somewhere remote, and we survived, it could take several days before we were found. We'd need to get that tent up, put on thermal clothing and get inside our arctic sleeping bags. But at night…bloody hell, it could be minus 50°C. If we got cold, we'd struggle to warm up again, especially if it was overcast and very cold the following day.

In Nepal, most of the days were sunny, so there was time to warm up, to dry our clothes. It's cold – sure – but it's sunny. It was actually funny at base camp on

Everest; when the sun set at around 4pm, there would be a mad rush as everybody ran back to their tents to dig out their thick down leggings and jackets. The whole camp would suddenly be on the move. As soon as the sun started setting, the temperature plummeted and I could watch the shadow moving across the valley like a dark shade coming down Pumori.

Out in northern Canada, it was unlikely we'd get any warmer weather to complement the cold. Plus, there would be no one else around – no support system like on Everest. We would be in full-on survival mode, hoping someone would find us before the polar bears did.

So we stocked up on as much food as we could carry at the supermarket. We were on our way back to the lodge when a truck went past that looked like a police car – the first sign of law enforcement we'd seen in the village.

When we arrived back, the owner approached us immediately.

'The police have been looking for you,' she said.

'What do they want?' I was alarmed. It can't have been the window, I thought. The owner didn't seem too put out by that.

When we'd landed in Pangnirtung, we'd said we'd only be there one night, but the weather had meant we'd had to stay on. Maybe that was it.

'They want to come and speak to you. I need to tell

them you're back.'

What might the police be like out here in the middle of nowhere, during the Covid pandemic when they hadn't had any visitors for weeks – and visitors weren't necessarily as welcome as usual? Fifteen minutes later, we heard a car crunch to a halt in the snow outside – the same one that had passed us as we returned from the supermarket. We were about to find out.

Two police officers strode in. Big lads, dressed in full black body armour including bullet-proof vests, with pistols in holsters on their hips. In the UK, if you saw police officers dressed up like that, you'd think they were going on a drug bust or to hunt down a known killer, not to question a couple of pilots stuck in town because of crappy weather. They were not Inuit, so had likely been stationed here. I could see from their badges that they were part of the Canadian Mounted Police, although there probably wasn't a horse within hundreds of miles.

Without any greeting, they started questioning us.

'Where are you from and what are you doing here?' asked the first one, who had a shaven head.

The other, slightly younger, stood with his big muscly arms crossed aggressively.

I explained the situation – how we were taking the helicopter back to Guernsey.

'We've seen the helicopter. Why are you still here?' asked the younger officer.

'The weather. We tried to leave this morning but the weather made us turn back.

'Why did you go into the village?'

'For supplies.'

I started to suspect that the main cause of concern was indeed Covid. They wanted to keep us contained somewhere away from the general population, which I could understand.

I pulled out my phone and showed them images of our negative Covid tests.

'I've got to send that on,' said the officer with the shaven head.

'Send it on to who?'

'The team, to verify. I need your phone so I can type in the email.'

A little confused, Martin and I both handed our phones over and the officer entered an email address for us to send copies of our Covid tests to. We hit send and they both noticeably calmed down a bit and became friendlier.

'So how long have you guys been policing up here?' I asked, still worried that we might be arrested and put in a cell.

'A couple years,' the younger one replied.

'It's very remote.'

He shrugged. 'You get used to it.'

I couldn't imagine a couple of years there. It was a fascinating place to visit, to drop in with a helicopter and check out, but actually living in Pangnirtung must be a very different experience. We'd had a taste of it, and the villagers were very friendly – with the possible exception of Mr Pessimist – but I wouldn't have wanted to stay for much longer.

'And you?' I asked the one with the shaven head.

'I'm holiday cover,' he said.

'Holiday cover?'

'There are three Inuit villages around here. I'm up here for cover.'

I was surprised. 'Is there much need for policing in these villages?'

He nodded. 'Oh yeah.'

'How come?'

'Alcohol. Everyone gets drunk, then they all fight. That's the main issue.'

This made sense. I remembered being told that alcohol had had a large negative impact on the Inuit population when they were first introduced to it. Alcoholism was rife and, with the long nights and freezing temperatures, I wasn't entirely surprised to learn there could occasionally be trouble.

'Do you ever need backup?' I asked.

'It's a two-hour flight away,' the officer shrugged.

'You're on your own then.'

'If we have to call for backup, we head for the police station and lock ourselves in the cells.'

This made me laugh, but he was dead serious.

'Do any of the locals have guns?' I continued, beginning to think the situation through.

He nodded. 'They've all got them.'

Three villages full of people with guns, who get violent when they drink too much. I was beginning to see why this pair were so fully kitted-up.

'Worst thing is that we've got no idea how many guns there are, because none of them have licences.'

'Is it legal to have a gun without a licence here?'

He shook his head firmly. 'What happens is, the grandfather hands a gun down to the father, who hands it down to a son. Everyone thinks they've got the right to have these guns to protect themselves against polar bears. But that's not what they end up being used for.'

I could see the officers' point. If an entire community ignores a law, how could these two men do anything about it? Especially when they're effectively considered outsiders. Every house had a gun and these policemen knew that. Every bar fight had the capacity to turn deadly. It sounded as if the whole place was like a tinderbox. I wouldn't want to be in their shoes if things started to get out of hand.

We chatted with the two officers a little while longer before they bade us good day and wished us luck, satisfied by our promises that we would be leaving the next day, weather permitting.

By this point, it was only around two o'clock and the afternoon stretched out ahead of us with nothing to fill it. I contemplated going down to the harbour, as I'd seen a couple of little boats go out and I wondered whether somebody would be willing to take me along. I liked the idea of heading up the fjord with them for the day, fishing or whatever they were doing.

In the end, I was too knackered. I'd been up for nearly twelve hours and I didn't have the energy. I decided I probably needed a day of doing nothing, after all the flying I'd already done, to build up my strength and concentration for the crossing to Greenland.

Towards the end of the evening, I woke to the sound of someone speaking French. A woman was seated on the sofa nearby with her two kids.

We started chatting and it turned out they were up in Pangnirtung to visit family, as she was part Inuit. So the place wasn't completely without visitors – but the five of us were the only occupants of the lodge, which had some thirty rooms.

The kids were obviously very excited, running around the lounge. This was clearly their big family holiday for the year.

'Can I give them a Mars Bar each?' I asked.

'Of course,' their mother said. 'They love them. But it will be a nightmare for me later on. They will be buzzing for hours on end.'

I laughed. I knew what it was like from when Steph and Lizzie were young. I handed the Mars Bars out to the kids. They looked more excited than ever and scoffed them at top speed.

It was getting late, so I said goodnight to the family and went to my room. We intended to follow the same early-start plan in the morning, in the hope that the weather would be better and we'd be able to get over to Greenland this time.

Despite a day of napping, I fell asleep almost immediately – but I didn't stay asleep for long. When dishing out the Mars Bars, I hadn't realised the French-speaking family were in the room next to mine. And the mother wasn't wrong about the kids. They were literally bouncing off the walls – shouting, racing around the room, jumping on the beds. The walls weren't exactly soundproof and it sounded like they were jumping on the bed I was trying to sleep in.

Every time I was about to nod off, there'd be another bang, another kid bashing into my wall. After about an hour of this, I had to say something. I went and knocked on their door, bleary-eyed.

The mother opened the door.

'I'm sorry, but I need to get some sleep, we've got an early start tomorrow. So, would it be possible to keep the kids quiet?'

'You see, this is what happens with Mars Bars.'

'Yeah, I'm regretting that now.'

I returned to my room, put my earplugs in, changed to the bed on the other side of the room and fell straight to sleep. This time, fortunately, I slept all the way through until morning.

I woke early and met Martin in the lounge for a second attempt at the Greenland crossing.

'A bit better today,' said Martin.

I looked out of the window.

'Yeah, a little bit,' I agreed.

The weather still wasn't great, but it looked like we might have a clear tunnel through the low-lying cloud.

I left Martin to his breakfast, got my stuff together, dropped our room keys at reception once more, and went to check the helicopter. Thinking about the flight to Greenland, I remembered the story of Sergey Ananov, a Russian helicopter pilot who attempted it in 2015, in a Robinson R22 – the same helicopter in which I'd learned to fly.

Ananov flew across the Davis Strait, from Iqaluit to Nuuk in Greenland. Everything was looking good for him. He'd flown over Canada, which had all gone well, and by all accounts he was pretty confident – to the extent that, because the cockpit was so hot and sweaty, he had his dry suit peeled down to his waist. Then the engine cut out without warning. He went down.

He was now fighting with the controls in autorotation so his hands and feet were busy trying to glide the helicopter down (this is actually possible, as the blades keep turning, like a sycamore-tree seed spins as it falls). There was no time to zip up; he just had to concentrate on the controls and pray. He aimed for an iceberg, missed it by about 40 feet and went straight into the freezing sea. The water poured into the helicopter immediately and it began to sink. The water also went straight into his suit, yet he still managed to zip it up and then get out of the now deadly hulk of metal.

He cleared the helicopter as it submerged, but dived back down again to pull out his life raft. He successfully inflated it then paddled across what I imagine must have felt like an endless ocean to the iceberg. He crawled out onto the ice, dragging the life raft behind him. At this point, he had to take off the dry suit and completely strip to get rid of all the freezing salt water inside it.

Somehow, he managed to do all of this without going hypothermic. Even with a dry suit on, you won't survive long in the water. It's going to be staggeringly cold. This guy should have had literally minutes to live, but he managed to do all that and then put the dry suit back on. He would still have been absolutely freezing and standing on a block of ice.

What then? He was stranded on an iceberg in the middle of the ocean, with his helicopter and comms equipment sinking to the seabed. He ended up staying on the iceberg for two days, sleeping under his life raft and surviving on what meagre rations he had. Supposedly, a couple of polar bears came up to have a sniff at him in the night, but he waved his hands at them, made a lot of noise and they went away again.

On the third day, through the fog, he saw the dull outline of a ship sent to find him. He had one flare left. He let it off in the direction of the shadow. One person on board saw the flare and alerted the captain. One person saw it – without that person, he would have died on that iceberg – and he was rescued.

Even thinking about it made me shiver.

10
WAY TOO HIGH

Not a soul stirred in the village and it was bitterly cold – minus 10°C again. I plodded back up the hill to the runway. The fog was definitely a bit better, as I could actually see further than the end of my nose.

When I arrived at the helicopter, I carried out a full check. I checked the oil levels, transmission oil, engine oil, hydraulic fluid and the tail-rotor gearbox oil. All those oil levels are critical, because if you haven't got enough, the gears will seize and the helicopter could drop out of the sky. My policy is always oil first. I did the full flight check, but triple-checked the oil. The thought of the turbine engine seizing up mid-flight filled me with dread.

I also checked all the hydraulic arms. It's a powerful helicopter and hydraulic fluid runs the whole show, with little servos that actually move the blades when you do a movement with the cyclic in the cockpit. It's just like power steering in a car – except twenty times more expensive, because it's aviation and supposedly built not to fail.

Whenever I carry out a flight check on a helicopter, I'm always amazed by its rudimentary nature. This helicopter isn't fly-by-wire, so there aren't electronic motors controlling the mechanics in the tail, as is the case with big commercial planes. You move the stick in the cockpit, which moves some rods under the floorboards. They run right up the back behind the rear seats. You can actually see the rod coming up where it connects to the hydraulic servo system, so whatever move you make, the servo boosts it by twenty times with hydraulic fluid pressure, and then that rod comes back out again and goes straight up to the blade. It really is that simple – and hence reliable and resilient.

The great thing about this simplicity is that there's no reliance on a computer system to keep it running. In those big planes, if the computer goes wrong, you're probably stuffed. Fly-by-wire helicopters are also very scary for exactly the same reason.

On the Bell 505, if the hydraulics fail, you can still fly it. It is bloody hard to fly, of course, because the steering becomes incredibly heavy, but it is flyable. They make you practise doing this when you learn to fly. There's a switch on the dash to turn off the hydraulics and suddenly it's your job to land without the hydraulic power-steering – it's like controlling a flying brick. It feels like you need to be Arnold Schwarzenegger: the controls are so heavy. You can't get the refinement of movement you need to put it down gently, so you come in to land and sort of skid it along the ground, knowing full well that if you screw that up and slide one way or the other, you'll tip the whole thing over, the blades will smash and it will be messy – very messy. And, if you survive, very expensive.

I finished the flight check, had a look to see whether everything had been refuelled as requested, and I was ready to go.

Standing by the side of the helicopter, trying to keep out of the snow, I pulled on my heavy orange dry suit. At least that made me feel a bit warmer.

I saw Martin appear in his dry suit, traipsing through the snow in the morning twilight.

'Ready for this?' I asked.

'As I'll ever be,' he said.

It was quite scary to be leaving Canada and heading to Greenland. OK, we were in Pangnirtung, which was remote and very far north, but if there was a problem while I was flying in Canadian airspace, Canadian rescue services would come to our aid. Even though we were two hours from any form of civilisation, I knew the emergency services would be there if there was a crisis, and they would go into action to help us.

Greenland, on the other hand, is a huge country, the size of Europe, but with a population of only 60,000.

WAY TOO HIGH

They just don't have the resources to go out and help two idiots trying to fly a helicopter from Canada to Guernsey. They're not going to be able to mobilise an army to come and find us. It's not going to happen.

This was the biggest step I'd so far taken into the abyss. Martin and I were really on our own from this point on, whenever we were in the air. Any problems? We'd have to deal with them ourselves.

I jumped into the pilot seat, and Martin climbed into the co-pilot's place beside me. I fired up the helicopter, lifted into a hover and made my way back on the route that had defeated me the day before. I climbed up the steep 500ft cliff, over the mountain top and headed towards the fjord on the other side – all good. I then headed up the fjord. There was another mountain to cross at the end before we reached the open sea, the large expanse of Baffin Bay between Canada and Greenland.

It looked clear enough so we climbed up over the far end of the fjord, the Bell 505 performing beautifully. The cloud was patchy, drifting up and down. This was disturbing. Might it suddenly envelop us, in every helicopter pilot's nightmare? After a while I spied the far end of the mountain ridge and the foggy open sea beyond.

I'd done a weather forecast in the morning, using satellite images, so I knew the cloud was going to be up at 9,000ft. As a result, I had made the decision to go over the fog, not under it. If I kept above it, there should be blue skies and sunshine. Then I would just need to find a hole in the cloud to drop through once we were over Greenland, and we'd have 25 minutes of contingency fuel to do it.

But first I needed to get above the clouds. I saw a gap and shot towards it, climbing steeply, up, up and away, praying that I wouldn't get enveloped by the surrounding clouds.

The 505 performed like a dream. It has a great power-to-weight ratio so it climbed very rapidly – 5,000ft, 6,000ft, 7,000ft. Come on cloud; just keep that window open for me – 8,000ft, and bang… Out into the sunshine at 9,000ft. It was glorious up there. The sun shone brightly and it lifted my spirits. Flying above the clouds in the clear sunshine was easy.

Back at Mirabel, the Bell pilots had told me that if I flew higher I'd fly faster, as the air was thinner, and if I could get into a westerly jet stream (tailwind), that would also blow us along our route. We would burn less fuel too.

So that's what I did, taking the helicopter further up than we had been before to try to maximise our fuel reserves and avoid the cloud. But the thinness of the air presented a problem. There was no pressurisation in the helicopter, and no oxygen. It's not like a 747 crossing the Atlantic, with nice, pressurised cabins, oxygen masks, heating systems and numerous emergency safety devices to keep it flying. It's literally a glass bubble with an engine strapped to it, and the only source of heat we had came from the bleed air system, as it pushed the heat from the engine into the cockpit.

But it was still better to be up there than the alternative. The forecast showed that, other than a 200ft to 500ft gap between the sea and cloud, it was fog all the way up to 9,000ft. We had debated whether it would make sense to fly under the fog, closer to the sea, in case I had to make an emergency landing on an iceberg. But we were due to fly for four and a half hours. What if at some point in all that time the gap suddenly closed up? I would get disorientated very quickly and within minutes lose control and crash into the sea. A height of 200ft may sound big, but when you're flying an aircraft at 150mph, it's peanuts. Any over-movement of the controls and you've just descended 300ft...into the sea. That would be game over for Martin and me.

So, I opted for the sunshine.

Of course, there were still risks. I had to hope I'd find a gap in the freezing fog over Greenland through which we could descend and land. If I had to fly down directly through freezing fog, bad and potentially fatal things could happen. But I would worry about that in four and a half hours. For the time being, I was just enjoying the view – and feeling a bit lightheaded with the lack of oxygen at 9,000ft.

Breathe in, breathe out. Deep breath in. The air was getting noticeably thinner.

'How are you, mate?' I asked Martin.

'Yeah, it's getting thin.' He gulped at the air.

It was getting colder too. It gets colder as you rise up in the air – roughly two degrees for every 1000ft. But we had to keep going upwards, because the cloud ahead started to rise. We lifted up to 10,000ft. The cloud ahead rose again. If it went on like this, we would eventually pass out due to lack of oxygen. I was now really starting to worry: the forecast had said cloud tops of 9,000ft max for that day – but it had been wrong. I climbed again over the rising clouds to 11,000ft, then 12,000ft, then 13,000ft.

This was getting really bad.

And, again, I had to rise – to 14,500ft. It was now extremely cold – minus 14°C – and I was having to breathe very heavily to stay focused. The heater wasn't keeping me warm.

Finally, the cloud stopped rising. We were lucky: God must have been watching us.

After about an hour of speeding across the alien cloudscape beneath us, my thoughts turned to fuel. We'd need to use the fuel sack to make sure we made it across the water.

'Can you try the fuel pump?' I asked Martin.

'It's already on,' he replied.

With my headsets and all the noises of the helicopter, I couldn't hear the pump motor. 'Is it working?'

'Jesus, I hope so.'

I put my hand behind me and felt for the pump. It was vibrating gently. That was good – at least it was operating. I had to hope it was also pumping fuel. I looked at the gauge; it was looking pretty full. Again, relief washed over me. We were nearly at the go/no-go point where we'd have to turn back if it wasn't working.

I looked down again at the fuel gauge. It seemed the fuel sack was pumping in at the same rate that we were using up the fuel. A lot rested on that little pump, especially when we passed the halfway point of our day's flying. And of course the fuel pump was plugged into the cigarette-lighter socket. As I'd already realised before we started this journey, there was always the risk of the fuse tripping out, in which case we wouldn't be able to reset it. A lot was riding on that little fuse, as well as the pump. We had no choice but to keep our fingers crossed and hope for the best.

I told myself I was in danger of ruining the whole experience by allowing my mind to get stuck on something like a fuse. We were doing something utterly extraordinary – cruising along above rolling clouds in crisp blue skies, in a part of the world where very few people will ever have the chance to fly an aircraft. People don't normally fly helicopters at 14,500ft, as we were doing. In the UK, most general aviation involves flying at around 2,000ft. You can see everything on the ground. You can see the houses, you can see the sheep, you can see the fields, you can see everything. You can also see where you can land in an emergency. But we were right up with the gods – all we could see was the clouds beneath us. With the tail wind, we were whizzing along with a ground speed of 190mph.

And I was thinking about the damned fuse.

But it was hard not to. My mind dwelled on all the ways in which this splendidly serene scene might turn into the last thing I ever saw – in the blink of an eye. Everything seemed so settled and calm but I was acutely aware that the potential for real and immediate danger was ever-present.

Even the clouds – which looked magical, as soft and harmless as candy floss – were deadly. They were actually trapping us at that great height. Because the temperature was below freezing, if we dropped down into them, the windscreen would frost up immediately, the blades would start to build up hoar frost on the leading edge and everything would start to freeze. As ice built up on the blades, the aircraft would become very unstable, very quickly. It would start shuddering like crazy, then the blades would fail and we'd drop like lead out of the sky.

That, inevitably, made me start wondering what it would be like to fall 14,500ft out of the sky. You'd have a few seconds to think about it before you hit the sea. What would I do? Would I jump out of the door – hoping I could somehow survive the drop into the sea, while also hoping I didn't hit an iceberg on landing? Would I sit in the aircraft and hope to hell that when I crashed into the sea it didn't kill me? From this height, it almost certainly would. What would Martin do?

I guess we would soon find out if any of that actually happened. I was now so committed to our course that there was nothing we could do but ride it out. If this machine failed now, if it ran out of fuel, if there was a problem with the pump, if that fuse packed in, we'd be dead. If the engine did fail, I could disconnect the engine by pushing down the collective lever, and float down and steer. But not if we went into freezing fog and ice built up on the blades, making them unstable. They'd eventually rip themselves off. Once they were out of balance, they were not going to last long, even on a fabulous machine like the Bell 505.

In many ways, I felt I was in more danger than at any point when climbing Everest. Granted, in the death zone (above 26,000ft) there was very little chance of rescue if something went wrong – if you fell into a crevasse or passed out – but there was still a small chance. Up above the clouds, in the helicopter, we were totally isolated for five hours, in a little glass bubble with a single engine. If anything went wrong, we'd have no way of getting out.

It really was total commitment. It was go under the clouds or go over, and I'd committed to going over them. I was totally reliant on the aircraft.

'Right,' I said. 'I think it's time for a sarnie.'

Martin took over the controls while I dug about in my bag and pulled out a squashed sandwich. I had a flask of tea next to me, so I poured myself a cup and stuck some music on via the iPhone. A bit of distraction to help me forget the insanely precarious position we were in.

I sat there, looking out over the cloud, munching on a sandwich and enjoying a cuppa. It was a little moment of calm, even though I had a perpetual knot in my stomach.

'We'd better see if we can get hold of somebody – let them know we're not dead yet,' I said.

We'd been flying for a couple of hours by now and I was supposed to call in every half an hour to let Greenland and Canada know we were OK. I'd been struggling with the Bluetooth satellite phone throughout the trip, making it very tricky to make a call, and the helicopter radio was too weak to reach anybody out where we were, so we were totally dependent on the sat phone for communication.

I fiddled with its settings, picked up some static on my headset. Then it went dead. Could I get the Bluetooth to work, to link my helicopter headset to the sat phone? Could I, hell. It was impossible.

I took the sat phone out of the Bluetooth docking station, removed my headset from one ear, punched in the number for Sisimiut airport and stuck the phone to my head.

'Hello? Can you hear me? Hello?'

One thing about helicopters is that they're bloody noisy. I've got a great Bose A20 noise-cancelling headset. You press a button for noise-cancelling and… zhuuuuuum, everything closes out – all the outside noise, the blades, the engine, all high-frequency and low-frequency stuff is cut out. It's really mind-blowingly good…until you take the headphones off.

'November Five Zero Five Hotel here. Radio check!' I shouted into the phone.

Very distantly, I could hear the faintest response, almost lost among the helicopter noises. I had no idea what the person on the other end was saying. I continued to shout. It was ridiculous – like something out of a Monty Python sketch. I had the phone glued to my ear but I couldn't hear a thing.

'We're fine, we're fine,' I shouted. 'We're on track. All good! I can't hear you… I've got to go now.'

I hung up, hoping they'd got the message.

'We made contact,' I said to Martin. 'That's the main thing.'

I took over the helicopter controls again and we ploughed onwards.

Not long afterwards, a voice came through the

headset. It sounded like comms from a commercial plane, somewhere above us. I didn't know if it was Greenland Air or someone else, but I could try radioing them and asking if they could relay a message to Sisimiut Airport in Greenland for us.

'This is November Five Zero Five Hotel, radio check. Do you read me?' I said.

'Roger November Five Zero Five Hotel. We hear you,' a voice replied.

I relayed my request, asking them to tell Sisimiut Airport where we were, to let them know we were making good progress and should be with them in a couple of hours. The commercial pilot was more than happy to use his more sophisticated comms systems to get the message across, and I relaxed a little, knowing that Sisimiut wouldn't be sounding the alarm and assuming we'd crashed into the ocean.

It was all looking good: the fuel pump was keeping our fuel topped up; our destination knew we were on route, and I'd had a cup of tea. I was actually starting to enjoy myself.

'BEEP BEEP BEEP!!! BEEP BEEP BEEP!!!' wailed an electronic alarm suddenly, accompanied by a red light flashing 'WARNING WARNING'.

Holy shit!

11
THE RED ZONE

'Jesus! What's that?' said Martin.

'BEEP BEEP BEEP! ECU DEGRADE!'

The incessant alarm cut like a knife – a piercing, shrieking noise. The clouds seemed to yawn in front of us, ready to cast us to our deaths in the ocean.

'*Damn!*' I said. The ECU was the electronic control unit. 'Degrade isn't good.'

'Shit! What do we do?'

'I'm trying to think.'

This aircraft had over fifty possible error messages, and I had to remember them in my head – all fifty of them. Bollocks, what was this one? Were we about to drop out of the sky?

'BEEP BEEP BEEP! ECU DEGRADE.'

The aircraft continued to scream in our ears, crying out about the bloody ECU.

'It's telling us it has detected a malfunction in the

engine controls system,' I said after a moment.

'Probably because it's so bloody cold. It's minus 14°C,' said Martin.

'If we fly carefully, fly straight and don't make any violent movements, we should be OK and we should land as soon as is practical. Mind you, that's not going to be for an awfully long time.'

I'm not sure I sounded wholly convincing but when the computer system that controls everything fails, the fuel valves can stop at the level they were last at. What that could mean is that when you try to set the aircraft on the ground, you're pumping too much fuel into the engine.

'It could be difficult when we come in to land,' I said.

'If we come in to land,' replied Martin, sounding just a little less than his usual cool self.

My thinking was that if we flew gently, carefully – kept going and got to Greenland – we could worry about how we put the helicopter down when we got there. The engine might over-rev when we started to land, as it could still be pumping fuel like mad, but in theory we could put it down without a disaster.

I pressed the mute button to shut the ECU degrade alarm. The danger message stayed on the screen in front of me, a bright-red blinking reminder that I might just be pushing my luck too far.

I grabbed the packet of wine gums next to me. Whenever I got a bit nervous during the trip, I'd taken to chewing wine gums. Right now, I was piling them in, chewing like mad. Moving the headset mic down, chucking a wine gum in; mic back up again, chew, chew, chew; mic back down, chuck a wine gum in, chew, chew, chew. It was something to focus on other than the bloody ECU degrade.

Twenty minutes passed and we were thankfully still airborne. I'd started to relax a little, easing up on the wine gums.

'My feet are having a hard time,' said Martin.

That was when he reached for the heating knob to try and increase the temperature in the cabin and it spun uselessly in his hand.

'BEEP BEEP BEEP! COLD BATTERY, COLD BATTERY! BEEP BEEP BEEP!'

So now we had a broken heating control, ECU degrade and a frozen battery. And my wine gum supply was dwindling.

'BEEP BEEP BEEP!' went the warning system again. This was the third warning. It felt like the final straw.

I'd pushed it all my life, I thought to myself. I was a cat with nine lives and I'd already used up ten of them. This was it. I'd pushed it too far this time. I should never have done this trip. I didn't even know why I was doing it. And now I was going to die. What was it even for? I thought of my lovely daughters.

'BEEP BEEP BEEP!' screamed the alarm again.

Wait, what was that? Yes, of course. The battery has

a built-in heater – a smart printed circuit board – and if the battery started to get cold, the heater would warm it up. And it was bloody working.

I dared to breathe a little sigh of relief. This warning was a good warning, telling us the cold battery was sorting itself out. It was a really, really smart bit of tech – something you don't get in the old helicopters. Nothing like it.

That was bloody marvellous. The battery wasn't going to be the problem that killed us. I had no idea how long it would take to warm up fully, but I prayed it wouldn't fail. If it did fail, we'd lose all the electronics and – up at 14,000ft in minus 14°C – it would not be pretty.

If all the electronics failed, we did have a little standby unit called SAM with its own battery. That would keep working for 30 minutes, but all we'd get on the screen in front of us would be the altitude and speed. The bare minimum. Two little tiny dials at the top.

Relying on those two dials in these conditions, at that height with another two hours of flying? No thanks. It didn't feel good. Luckily, it was now looking as if we wouldn't have to do that, if the battery warming circuit did its job.

I kept flying – and flying and flying; there was nothing else I could do. It may have been bloody cold but at least up there the skies were blue, we could see clearly ahead and the sun was shining.

Still, the only thing keeping me going – keeping me from panicking – was that I had a job to do that required my full attention. I had both feet going, both hands going; I was concentrating hard. There was music pumping through the headset now, calming my frayed nerves. That's what I needed. The concentration it took to pilot the helicopter, to do the job at hand, kept my mind off the fact that we could die at any minute. If anything else failed, we would most likely not make it.

I was dimly aware that it must be even worse for Martin. Despite his unrufflable exterior, he had nothing to do but worry, with his fate completely out of his own hands.

On we ploughed; on and on and on. And then, of course – my body had been twitching and twisting for three hours, I was very nervous, full concentration – nature called! Even if you're flying thousands of feet over the freezing ocean in a glass bubble that might fall apart at any moment, it does still do that, and I was dying for a pee. It seemed the helicopter wasn't the only thing struggling with a crossing of this length.

There was nothing I could do about it. There was no toilet on the aircraft and, even if there had been, I couldn't get out of my seat. There was nothing for it but to hold on.

The cloud rolled below us, thick freezing and uninviting. It was an inhospitable blanket, stretching to the horizon. I prayed that when we got closer to Greenland and the land rose up over the polar ice cap, there would be some holes in the cloud cover through which we could safely drop. I'd checked out the coastline on the satellite images that morning and it looked as if we might be in luck, but those images never give you the full picture. The holes in the clouds could be much smaller than anticipated, and they could have closed up at any point in the last four and a half hours. These risks were very real.

For four and a half hours we'd been sitting absolutely still, deep in concentration. My bum was really starting to get sore. It really is the most minute movements that control the helicopter – the lever between the legs, the cyclic, the collective lever, plus the two pedals. You have to be in complete control of all of them at all times. If you stretch – push your foot out – the whole bloody helicopter swings around. For all that time I'd stayed dead still, apart from those barely perceptible movements to correct our course.

Now I found myself feeling fidgety. I badly needed to get out of that glass bubble, that Perspex death box. Focus, I told myself; concentrate. Don't think of anything else but getting this beautiful creation across this ocean.

My mobile phone pinged. Then another notification ping, then another.

'What the hell is that?' Martin asked.

'I don't know how, but I seem to have a phone signal,' I said. We were at least twenty miles from land, way off the coast, but there I was, getting messages through to my phone. 'I guess we should give Sisimiut a call.'

'Go for it.'

Sure enough, the Bluetooth link from my mobile phone was working perfectly – it was the sat phone link that wasn't.

I punched in the number for the airport. The phone rang a few times before it was answered, the line crystal-clear.

'Um, hi,' I began, giving our call sign. 'We're en route – should be with you in around thirty minutes.'

'We're expecting you,' a voice replied.

The weight that had been on my shoulders for most of the flight started to lift, the knot in my stomach loosened. Just hearing another voice telling me that we were expected made it feel like this hellish flight was nearing an end. If we could only find a way through that wall of cloud, we might even survive it.

'You're lucky,' the voice said. 'The cloud is clearing a bit. You should be able to find a way through.'

I thanked him, docked the phone again and gave Martin a big smile.

'All good. The cloud is lifting; never in doubt,' I said nervously.

We trucked along for a little while longer and then we saw it in front of us – a big hole in the cloud. I felt a surge of relief and I finally began to ease us down through that gap, which ushered us into a different realm. The complete desolation and other-worldliness of the vacuum above the clouds was replaced by an incredible panorama, seemingly erupting from the ocean. The Greenland coast rose before us like an oasis in the desert. The explosion of colour – deep greens, dark browns, vivid whites – was in marked contrast to our monochromatic view of the past few hours: white fluff below and blue sky above.

Time for a very small celebration. I stuck on The Beatles to give a little fanfare to the occasion. 'The Long And Winding Road' – sung beautifully by Paul McCartney – seemed an appropriate song and lifted my heart. We were going to make it; we were going to make Greenland.

The town of Sisimiut is located on an inlet on the vast island's western coast, with the main town to the south and the airport just across the estuary to the north. We had a magnificent sweeping view of the whole place, the colourful yellow, red and blue buildings with their steeply pitched roofs looking like something out of a Hans Christian Andersen fairy tale. A covering layer of snow made these small pinnacles of colour even more striking.

We flew straight towards the town, and the airport soon came into view to the left of us.

'Any idea where we land?' asked Martin.

'Not a clue.'

I radioed up the tower and they guided us in. Even with the ECU degrade, the helicopter handled well. I eased the collective lever down carefully and the helicopter responded. There was a single runway with another plane on it which we flew around before popping our aircraft down not far from the tower, about 20 metres from the barbed-wire perimeter of the airfield.

We put on our Covid masks and gloves and jumped out for a hugely welcome stretch of the legs. This section of the journey had undoubtedly been the most gruelling so far, both mentally and physically.

I looked up at the sky. The weather had been iffy for a few days, and we'd managed the crossing in pretty crap weather. Here in Greenland, however, it had brightened up a bit. I could see the sun shining brightly through the hole in the clouds that had been our life-saver. As the weather front hit the steep coastal cliffs of Greenland it pushed the clouds up and created a clearer area above us.

'Let's keep going after we've refuelled,' I said. I knew worse weather was forecast for the next few days, so it made sense to make hay while the sun shone.

Martin nodded, cracking his back and stretching. It felt like the right call to both of us. After flying for four and a half hours we were knackered, but we needed this weather window. It was better to press on and fly over Greenland while we could.

The refuelling team arrived and started pumping the fuel into the helicopter and the fuel sack. We'd need to be fully topped up again because it was another four hours of flying to fly over the polar ice cap and get to the east coast of Greenland. Remember: Greenland is the size of Europe and it wasn't a short distance.

In a way, I felt a pang of sadness at the decision. I would have loved to stay the night in Sisimiut. In my mind, when planning the trip, I'd wanted to stay in Sisimiut, and then fly down to Nuuk, the capital of Greenland. Eighteen thousand people live there – a third of the population of the whole country – but I knew next to nothing about the place. Did they have any built-up areas? How cosmopolitan would it be? Frustratingly, I would never find out.

Of course, I wouldn't have been able to find out even if we weren't trying to make up time, because we were also in the middle of the Covid pandemic. It would have been irresponsible for us to visit Nuuk, and risk unwittingly introducing the virus to this isolated community, when it wasn't absolutely necessary.

As refuelling progressed, I made my way to the control tower to show our passports and pay for the fuel. I was greeted by the man I'd spoken to earlier over the radio. He wore a mask and kept his distance.

'It's a Sunday,' he said.

I was a little knocked by the abruptness.

'Yeah?' I said.

'I'm afraid there's a fee for landing on a Sunday. A thousand dollars.'

'You've got to be kidding.'

'And a handling fee.'

'Really?'

He nodded.

I looked out of the window at the runway, at the big Greenland Air commercial airplane that was sitting there.

'Those guys landed on a Sunday,' I said.

'They've got to pay as well.'

'That's a bit steep. You're manning the airfield, the control tower and the fuel truck because of those guys.'

'That's the rule.'

I thought there was no way those big, commercial jets were paying. They're not going to get billed for it. Just me. But also, there wasn't much I could do. These guys could pluck whatever number they wanted out of mid-air. So I paid up.

'If you'd landed on the other side of the barbed-wire fence, you wouldn't have been charged. That's not part of the airfield,' he said.

'I guess we couldn't have refuelled there though,' I said, trying my best to look on the bright side.

'No, we could have got the fuel truck to you if you'd landed just outside the fence.'

Wow, thanks, I thought to myself. The cheeky bugger

could have mentioned that to me as we were flying in.

Biting my tongue, I left the control tower and made my way back to the helicopter, which the team had finished refuelling.

'All good?' said Martin.

'Apart from the daylight robbery – we're on bread and dripping tonight, mate.'

We hopped back into the cockpit and prepped to take off. I was hoping, now that we had shut down and were about to re-start, that the ECU degrade message would disappear. I knew the battery had warmed up and was fine now. We now knew that the heater knob was stuck on windscreen de-mist, which was the better of the two options. We just had to put up with cold feet until we reached Iceland, where we would meet the Bell engineers.

I got clearance from the tower and started up the helicopter. I monitored all the controls and error messages. No ECU degrade warning – fantastic. All temperatures and pressures normal and no warning messages – we were good to go.

I listened to the comms and there was some debate as to who should go first – us or the plane on the runway. I looked a bit closer; it had a red cross on it.

'Is that a medical plane waiting to go?' I asked the tower.

'Yes,' crackled the reply.

'Look, it doesn't matter to us – we'll wait. Let them

go,' I said.

We waited there for fifteen minutes or so while the plane sorted itself out, taxied out onto the runway, did the necessary checks and took off. As soon as it had gone the tower cleared us and we lifted straight up and off on our next adventure – across the polar spine of Greenland.

12
ON THE POLAR ICE CAP

The cliffs were directly ahead of us – massive, awe-inspiring and rising almost vertically. The Bell 505 has the most amazing power/lift capabilities, so we were able to motor up the cliff face, straight into the air like a rocket. It felt fantastic, pulling on all those tonnes of jet power. We shot up over the top of the cliff and suddenly there was ice as far as the eye could see.

This was our first close-up sight of the polar ice cap, over which we'd be flying for the next four hours – another big leg. On this side of Greenland, the cap was scarred and rugged, due to the wind coming in from the west, ripping into it and creating deep gashes. There were holes in the surface, and deep blue veins crisscrossing beneath. The ice was smudged and dirty, due to the dust in the westerly wind. It looked like the rugged skin of a vast living being.

While I was trying to enjoy the view, the helicopter

decided the time had come to remind me of my mortality. The RPM warning light lit up on the dashboard, a big red beacon sitting in my peripheral vision.

This particular light normally comes on when the blade revolutions aren't sufficient, warning you that you're losing revolution speed and you're most likely going to be going down in the very near future. Nice.

I checked all the other dials. The turbine and the blades were both running at 106, which was spot on. Could it be another case of the cold getting to the aircraft? I decided to crack on. At least in emergency we could land on the ice. It wasn't like during the sea crossing, when it had been all or nothing.

Unless we met a polar bear, of course. The further inland we flew, the less likely this was, as the polar bears tend to stick to the coast, where their food sources (ie fish) are more prevalent. This is also where the main human settlements are located, again because of the same food sources, so polar-bear attacks are not infrequent.

I'd heard that the Inuit were only allowed to hunt and shoot mature male polar bears, that they'd be heavily fined if they shot female or young animals, as keeping population numbers steady was a serious concern. Personally I think the indigenous inhabitants of this region understand the native species better than we do. They know how many polar bears and seals they can safely kill while still allowing the population to continue to breed so that there will be enough for the year after and the year after that, for generations to come.

If the bears come into the villages, the women go out banging pots and pans, screaming and shouting to drive the animals away, and it works. The women are in charge of this because the higher pitch of their voices scares the polar bears more. For our part, we didn't have any pots and pans. We had a flare, but I'm not sure shooting a bear with a flare would be the best move; it might not kill the animal, and it might upset him a lot. If we found ourselves on the ground, it would probably be better to stay safely in the helicopter where the polar bears couldn't get to us.

The sun was now shining and the cloud had cleared as we flew over the polar ice cap. We were able to fly fairly low, as there were no obstacles to avoid, which gave me quite a rush. When you're 500ft up in the air, the ground below looks like it's moving very slowly. When you're close to the ground, it zips past underneath you at an alarming speed. It can be disorientating, and you have to concentrate very hard because the slightest mistake could be disastrous, but it was a phenomenal feeling.

Another bonus of flying over dry land is that we didn't have to wear the dreaded dry suits. I could move, I could breathe and I wasn't sweating in a

ON THE POLAR ICE CAP

horrible rubber suit any more. It was bloody cold but it was glorious nonetheless.

It took a while for it to dawn on me just how cold it was without the dry suit. It was minus 14°C outside, there wasn't enough heat from the heater, but I didn't really care. I was having the time of my life. Music was banging out through the headphones, we were zooming across this spectacular icy whiteness, the sun was now shining and I was thoroughly enjoying myself. This was what life – and flying – was all about.

A thought occurred to me.

'Shall we put her down?' I suggested. 'Get some photos on the polar ice cap?'

'Yeah, absolutely,' said Martin.

I slowed and landed in the middle of nowhere, whiteness in all directions as far as the eye could see. I

Standing on the polar ice cap in Greenland

reduced the revs to idle and slowly stepped out, testing the ground for firmness, ensuring I wasn't standing on a crevasse, the sound of my feet crunching in the snow like dynamite. Martin stayed in the helicopter, at the controls. The profound silence of the ice cap closed in around me as I stood there in the snow. The sound of my breathing was the only noise for miles, apart from the thud of the idling blades.

It was truly one of the most privileged moments of my life. I was probably the first human ever to stand on that exact spot. There was nobody within hundreds of miles of us. Civilisation, politics, Covid – all of it seemed to belong to a different world entirely. It was as if I'd flown the helicopter out of the earth's orbit and discovered a new world.

I thought about what it had taken to get there, to that exact point on the northern part of the earth's surface. I tried to recall what it felt like, taking off from Mirabel, or even further back, when I was at home, plotting a route on a map, a million miles from the reality of this biting wind, this gnawing, freezing chill.

I realised then that this was for me the adventure of a lifetime. This was the moment I'd look back on with the most pride; this was how I'd tell my story.

I hadn't understood quite what a huge risk this adventure would be when I was planning it – and I was cutting it closer and closer with every mad adventure I came up with – but this: this was what it was all about.

These tiny moments validated it all: the months of prep, the logistical hurdles, the naysayers who told me it couldn't be done; all of it.

I knew I was insanely lucky – that the chances of success were low and there was still a long way left to go before I could say the trip had been completed – but these are the kinds of challenges I love. I'd rolled the dice and it was worth it, because you are never more alive than when you are close to death.

I could have stood there for hours – days, even – just looking out across the icy arctic tundra, taking it all in. You get a unique perspective on the world when you're so far removed from it. Everything seems to become a little clearer when you're out of the hustle and bustle of everyday life, and you wonder why people are ever mean to each other on this beautiful planet.

But I also knew we had a mission to complete and couldn't dally too long, and we had to find somewhere to stay that night – no small task in these very remote places, especially in the age of Covid. It was time to go.

I took some photos but already I knew they would never quite do the experience justice.

I opened the door to the helicopter – a colossal noise in the dead silence. Every sound we made felt invasive, as if we were intruding on this quiet, content, terrifying landscape. It got worse as I revved the aircraft up. The blades spun up, louder and louder, disturbing the intense peace.

ARCTIC INSANITY

My world was full of noise and busyness again, each instrument on the helicopter sounding like a shotgun. I turned on the noise-cancelling function on my headphones and – phwoam – it sucked out all the background noise. Still, even then, I felt I would never be able to replicate the experience of calmness I had felt standing on the ice cap.

13
A BED FOR THE NIGHT

I took off into a hover, reluctant to leave. I turned the helicopter through 360 degrees to have one more look at that serene, snow-covered landscape, then I pointed the nose to the east, pulled on the power and we roared aloft, leaving our icy oasis of calm behind us.

I originally had a choice of destinations on the east coast: Kulusuk, which had a proper airport, or Ammassalik, which had a helipad.

In the end, I opted for Ammassalik, as I'd heard it was a nicer village, and larger. Also, I hadn't been there before, whereas I'd visited Kulusuk a few years previously on my ski-touring adventures.

We ploughed on for a couple of hours, the white landscape below us staying the same most of the way. As we neared the coast, however, the ice cap started to descend towards the sea. Unlike on the western coast, the ice was smooth here. It looked much cleaner, white and shiny, more serene and beautiful – like snow should look.

Soon afterwards, we started to spot signs of civilisation. Small man-made structures – hunting huts – appeared, and it was clear we were getting close to Ammassalik.

All the while, without realising it, I had been keeping my eyes out for movement in the snow. Camouflaged white rugs with tell-tale black noses. As we drew closer to humanity, I knew the chances of seeing polar bears were also increasing, as their territories and those of humans are intertwined. Polar bears and humans have essentially the same diet and needs. In the coastal habitat they share, there's plenty of hunting and plenty of food: fish, seals, whales and humans.

If you asked me whether I would like to live right in the middle of polar-bear territory, where the risks of getting eaten were high, I don't think I'd be rushing to take out a mortgage. But it makes sense, and there's not much choice anyway, because the hospitable coastal areas of Greenland are polar-bear heaven.

That's why villages like Ammassalik, based directly on the east coast of Greenland, right next to the sea, have developed. The Inuit have a strong maritime tradition, hunting seals and whales to survive. They're still allowed to hunt whales, because their impact on the overall whale population is very small. As with the polar bears, they're more in touch with the natural order of things than the rest of us. It's when industrialised nations come in with huge hunting ships and powered harpoons that things start to go wrong.

And who are we to tell the Inuit how to survive, how to live? For them, hunting whales and seals is their livelihood and way of life. If a load of other countries come together and declare, 'Oh no, you can't do this any longer – we've decided it,' what are the Inuit going to do? They have no option; this is how they survive throughout the year. If we don't want them doing that, we've got to give them something else that enables them to make a living.

Sadly, I didn't get a glimpse of a polar bear as we came in towards Ammassalik, but I am sure there were some beady eyes in the snow watching us.

Soon we were coming in over the village itself – small, beautifully colourful single-storey houses with corrugated roofs. The Inuit like their colour: yellow, blue, red and green houses sprinkled this plateau, right on the shore line. I flew towards the helipad, which was situated towards the southwest, near the coast.

I was still feeling the sting of that Sunday landing fee earlier in the day, and the guy telling me that if I'd landed just 20ft away, I wouldn't have had to pay, so I really didn't want to land on another helipad. Instead, I aimed at a patch of rough ground in a small clearing near the pad. They were not going to catch me twice in one day.

ARCTIC INSANITY

Below me, I could see some goats grazing, chewing at the grass all the way up to the spot where I planned to land. I didn't want them rubbing up against the aerials on the aircraft and damaging it, but I didn't have much choice. They scattered as I came in closer, gently bringing the helicopter onto the ground and shutting down the engine.

By now, it was nine o'clock at night, which was late to be trying to find somewhere to stay in such a remote

Safely landed at Ammassalik, late evening

area. I'd had a long day of flying – nearly ten hours, which is a lot in one day; ask any helicopter pilot – and we had no accommodation sorted.

I got out my phone which, to my amazement, pinged up with a 4G connection. I often struggle to get 4G at my own home, so it never ceased to amaze me when I could pick up such a strong signal out in the remotest parts of the world.

I googled 'accommodation in Ammassalik' and got a grand total of two results. Not to worry: if one said no, hopefully the other would say yes.

Martin and I picked up our bags and started walking up the hill towards the village. There had been nobody around at the helipad and associated buildings – the area was absolutely deserted – so presumably they'd closed for the night. Right now, our focus needed to be on finding somewhere to sleep.

We trudged through the slush along the side of a dirt road, slipping occasionally in our haze of tiredness. I kept my eyes glued to my phone, following the route up towards the first lodge we were going to try.

Suddenly we were hit by a blinding light, as if the sun had erupted early over the horizon. The beams lowered and a white car swooshed past. The only direction it could have been heading was the helipad.

'Hey, did that car have a taxi sign on top?' I said.

'That's what I was thinking,' Martin replied.

The headlights disappeared over a crest in the hill

and there were a few seconds of darkness again before it returned.

We flagged the car down and it was indeed a taxi – a surprising sight in this incredibly remote location, but a welcome one nonetheless. It pulled up next to us.

'Where do you want to go?' the driver asked, leaning out of the window.

'Can you take us to the Blue Lodge?' I said.

'Sure. Get in.'

We slid into the back of the vehicle, squashed in with our bags. I fought the urge to fall asleep immediately as the car took off up the road. There would have been no point anyway, because within minutes, we were at the front door of a long, one-storey blue building. We knocked and waited. Nothing. We knocked again, with no reply. On the door, a piece of paper had been Sellotaped, saying, 'If you arrive and nobody answers, ring this number.' I dialled, but the call rang off without an answer. I rang again and again but still no answer.

We waved at the taxi driver, who had been about to leave, and jumped back in his car. I asked him to take us back across town to the other lodge, back in the direction of the helipad. This one was called the Red House, and sure enough, it turned out to be a red house. They weren't very imaginative with their naming around here, but it made things very easy. The Red House was built on risers to keep it above the snow level. On the side of the building, UTILI

AAPALARTOQ (Red House) was printed in large white letters.

We paid the taxi driver, knowing this was our last hope if we weren't to spend the night huddled in the helicopter cockpit, and made our way up the wooden stairs to the door. I took a deep breath and knocked.

There was an excruciating thirty seconds of silence, and I'd just about given up hope when there was a shuffling sound from inside and a light came on.

I could hear the door being unlocked. It opened very slightly. A face with a shock of silver hair cautiously appeared.

'Yes,' the man said, in a strong Mediterranean-sounding accent. 'Can I help you?'

We'd grown used to seeing Inuit men and women over the past few days, with the occasional Dane, but if you didn't know any better you would swear that this man was Italian. His silver hair and olive complexion seemed very out of place in the snowy Arctic setting.

'Any chance we can stay for the night?' I asked.

'You need a bed?'

'Yes.'

'Bed?'

This does not look good. The man was clearly in no rush to make a decision. In fact, I wasn't even sure he could hear or understand me properly.

'Possibly,' he said. 'How did you come here?'

'Helicopter.'

'I saw it coming in. Are you pilots?'

'Yes. We're leaving tomorrow, taking the helicopter back to Europe.'

'They are very worried about Covid here.'

'Don't worry. We've had Covid tests. We're all clear.'

He took a moment to consider, sizing us both up, and then invited us in, opening the door wider, but making sure to step back.

I felt a big weight lift off my shoulders. Oh, for a comfortable bed for the night.

We stomped the snow and mud off our boots and walked into a large basic room with a wooden floor and a huge bookcase covering the entire back wall.

Hundreds of books were crammed onto the shelves, with rocks, shells and other items stuffed into the free spaces. Some simple chairs and tables made up the rest of the furnishings, in what looked like a dining room of sorts.

'Welcome to the Red House,' our host said. 'My name is Roberto.'

We dropped our bags and introduced ourselves, taking a look around the place. It was great – immediately homely and inviting.

There were some Inuit customers having a drink in the small annex linking the large dining room to the kitchen. As we approached, they immediately got up and left.

'I'm sorry,' I said. 'I hope we haven't made them

leave.'

'Everyone's worried about catching Covid,' Roberto said.

My stomach was growling like mad now.

'Do you have anything we could eat?' We hadn't eaten properly since breakfast fourteen hours earlier, and you burn through a surprising number of calories when you fly. With the adrenaline pumping you don't think about food. But now all that was behind us and we had beds for the night, we were both ravenous.

'No, I'm afraid we have finished dinner.'

'Have you possibly got a bit of bread or something – maybe a bit of toast?' I pleaded.

'With some cheese?'

'That would be fantastic!'

At that point, I didn't care what Roberto brought, I would eat it. A crusty old bit of bread with some processed cheese would feel like a lavish banquet.

We sat down at a window table near the kitchen and waited for our bread and cheese, too exhausted to talk.

Around ten minutes later, Roberto appeared with a platter. It was rye bread, with a fabulous smorgasbord of cheese and dried meats. There were two different types of Parma ham, both on the bone, as well as some pickle.

I was blown away. 'Where did you get all this stuff?'

'I'm Italian. We produce wonderful meats and cheeses. It's a passion of mine.'

I was wondering how the hell he got all this stuff out to Ammassalik, but I was too pleased to question it, for fear that it might disappear. Martin had already started slicing ham off the bone, like a gleeful child ripping into a Christmas present.

I felt that something was missing.

'I know it's pushing it a bit,' I said, 'but do you have any wine?'

Roberto lit up. 'I have some nice Italian bottles.'

He shuffled off into the kitchen and returned with a bottle of red and some glasses. He uncorked the bottle and poured us each a glass and then one for himself.

Leaning back in my chair, I was in heaven. What a great end to an extraordinary day!

'Tell me, what brings you out here?' I asked Roberto through a mouthful of cheese.

He took a sip of wine. 'That is a long story. The short version is that I run the Red House. It's a research centre. You saw the aerials outside?

'Yes. What are they for?'

'We're monitoring. There are other houses like this – one in Germany and one in Australia. Research scientists come here, and we analyse the state of the planet. It is quiet now, though.'

'Because of Covid?'

'That's right. We've had hardly any visitors this year. Normally, there will be a few teams; we will go up to the Mittivakkat Glacier – skin up on skis. But no expedition this year.'

Roberto sighed and stood up from the table. 'I will leave you for tonight. The weather doesn't look good for tomorrow. I expect you will be here longer than you'd hoped.'

He said goodnight and left us to finish our food.

'Sounds like it might be another no-fly day,' said Martin.

'Let's keep our fingers crossed we can go.'

Delicious bottle of wine finished, we retired contentedly to our bedrooms. The fact that I was far taller than the bed didn't bother me; I was so exhausted, I could have slept anywhere.

We'd crossed from Canada to Greenland over the polar ice cap and now there I was, sitting on the east coast of Greenland with an amazing snowy view out of the window down to the ocean. I felt I'd cleared one of the biggest hurdles of the trip and we were now nearly halfway there, with only one more major chunk of flying over isolated and remote regions left. We were heading south now; it was getting warmer and the weather was improving, so the danger quotient was also edging back down.

Still, the four-hour crossing over the freezing sea and icebergs to Iceland was bound to present more challenges and potential danger.

14
PARTY TIME

Still a little hazy from the wine, I pulled open the curtains the following morning to find that the colourful houses I had seen from my window the night before, the bay and the beautiful austere fjords around it had all been erased, replaced with a complete white-out.

This was really bad. The Red House was situated on a gentle slope, commanding panoramic views over the village and bay on a clear day, but not today. It was as if the building existed in total isolation, with nothing around it for miles and miles except white fog.

We were already two days behind schedule, and this was going to add to our delay. The two Bell engineers whom we were due to meet in Iceland had already flown out and were waiting there to give the helicopter a service it needed after 25 hours of flight. They were sitting in Reykjavik with nothing to do, waiting for us to arrive. I felt a little guilty. Still, I couldn't control the weather. And a weekend in Reykjavik? I reminded myself that there are far worse places to be stuck: a bit pricey for alcohol but it's a great little city, and I was sure those two Bell engineers would be making the most of their Icelandic jolly.

I got dressed and made my way out to the main room, where Martin was sitting glumly at the table.

'I know what you're going to say,' he said.

'You're right. No-fly day it is,' I said.

Roberto had laid breakfast, with more bread and cheese. They were both so good, I could have eaten them forever, so I was happy to tuck in.

After a short while, our host joined us.

'What will you do?' he asked.

'There's not a lot we can do,' I said. 'Would it be a problem if we stayed another night?' I really didn't fancy sleeping in the helicopter.

'Of course you can.'

'I'd like to have a walk around the village. Is there much to see?'

'Just a few shops. I'll draw you a map.'

He pulled out a small scrap of paper and scribbled on it.

'If you want souvenirs – postcards – you can go here,' he said, pointing at a location that he had marked 'big shop'.

I thanked him and tucked the map in my pocket.

'I must warn you though if you want to go outside the village, you need to tell me,' he added, his face dead serious.

'Oh?'

'I must make sure to come with you with a gun. It's the polar bears. Come, let me show you.'

Roberto led me through the dining area to a door in the wall, which opened into what appeared to be his office.

'Wow!' I exclaimed.

The walls were lined with cabinets, all of them brimming with guns. Shotguns, .303 rifles, a .308... he'd got the whole selection. It looked more like an armoury than an office.

'You've got some firepower here.'

'Sometimes it's needed. The bears have a great sense of smell. They smell the humans, smell the village. It's very tempting for them to come here if they get very hungry.'

I gulped. 'I'll definitely let you know if I want to leave the village.'

Becoming a snack for a polar bear wasn't exactly the way I had envisioned our expedition ending, and I thought back to the night before, when we were walking up the road from the airport at night. Had we been in real danger? I had no idea, but I was thankful that the only taxi in the village had found us.

Ten minutes later, I was crunching across the snowy

gravel into the village. The fog had lifted very slightly, so I could see further than the end of my nose, but visibility was still low and the fog played tricks on my eyes – every hut, car and building taking on the shape of a killer bear.

Compared to Pangnirtung, Ammassalik was light years ahead. It was the seventh largest settlement in Greenland. Although there were no roads outside the village – the only way of getting in or out was by sea or air – the infrastructure was more modern. I supposed the main reason was the influx of scientists every year, building up the town as they came and went.

I came across a takeaway in the main street. The idea of a takeaway out there on the east coast of Greenland

Heavy fog in Ammassalik – no flying today

seemed absolutely barmy to me – so much so that I had to try it.

I entered the building. It was quite busy, with a couple of local Inuit families sitting at the plastic tables and chairs, and a few workmen, who looked Danish, hanging out as well, sipping on cans of Coke and Fanta.

The menu offered a noodle special: prawn and fish. No burgers, no chips or anything else you might expect in a takeaway in the UK. I gave it a shot, but then realised this might not have been such a brilliant idea, given that I was scheduled to sit in a glass bubble over the sea for several hours the next day, with no escape or access to a loo.

It all made me wonder. You've got a supermarket, a takeaway, a post office, but how does it all fund itself? How does a village in the middle of nowhere keep going? Especially during a pandemic. Normally, I assume there would be big ships coming in. They would moor off the waterfront and tourists would visit the village. There was even a museum, which must cater to them. But now there was no sign of anybody. The people here had the seal and whale hunting to keep themselves alive, but the expeditions and tourist industry had completely died due to Covid.

In a heavily populated, industrialised country like the UK, the pandemic had had a huge impact on day-to-day lives, but the government had been able to introduce policies to try to support people;

whether they'd succeeded or not was another question entirely. But out here, I didn't know what they had in place, whether these people were just left to fend for themselves, despite their industry and livelihood collapsing overnight. They were practical and resilient, but I got the impression that the longer the Covid pandemic lasted, the more people living in remote parts of the world would suffer.

I left the takeaway and headed for the museum. I wanted to see what life was like in a town on the east coast of Greenland, and how it had changed over the years.

Inside, I found a workshop where local craftsmen were carving figures out of whale and seal bone. These were highly intricate figurines: chess pieces, necklaces, little things like that. They were on sale, but to whom? The Danish workers stationed in the village weren't going to buy them on a daily basis, and scientists like Roberto, who were there for the long haul, probably had enough of them by now to start their own shop. The closest thing Ammassalik had to a tourist just then was me. I got the impression those guys would still be sitting there long after we'd gone, waiting for tourists to return.

I bought a couple of trinkets for my daughters, then had a look around the museum. It was fascinating, with many traditional Inuit artefacts, including canoes, sledges and clothing. It's one thing to see these things

ARCTIC INSANITY

Ammassalik village with Inuit hunting sledge in the foreground

in the relative warmth of the British Museum, lodged among pieces from other cultures, also clamouring for attention. It was quite another to see them here in this frozen landscape, where they were made specifically to survive the sort of weather just outside the window.

Once I'd had my fill of the museum, I made my way back to the Red House. Not a polar bear in sight. I was struck by the sense that Greenland was a country caught between two worlds: between the reality of its existence here, with the bears and the seals and the snow, and the Danish outlook and mentality of the people.

When I arrived back, Roberto announced, 'We're having a big party tonight.'

'You are?'

'The locals like to cook. Some of them have asked to

use my kitchen for a party.'

'We'll stay out of the way.' I was conscious that some of the locals might be nervous about socialising with us due to Covid. Virtually everyone we had met since heading north in Canada, refuelling the helicopter and in lodge receptions and bars, had been Inuit, and they had almost all been very welcoming. But we didn't want to put anybody in an uncomfortable position.

'I'll speak to them to see whether you can join us.'

'I don't want to impose. If they don't want us around, we can stay in our rooms.' I didn't want to ruin their party. There had been nobody around for six months and we rock up on the day they're having a party! Good timing on our part, but terrible on theirs.

I passed the afternoon playing cards with Martin and flicking through some of the books from Roberto's well-stocked shelves. Our host had gone out again, rifle slung over his shoulder. He returned towards the end of the afternoon.

'I've spoken to them and they want you to join us for dinner,' he announced.

By this time I'd become more nervous than the locals about putting them at risk.

'That's really kind but I don't feel we can,' I said.

'But you must.'

'OK. We'll sit at another table well away from everybody so that we don't make anyone nervous.'

So that was the plan.

ARCTIC INSANITY

Roberto started moving items around the room, setting up a massive table by the windows, with at least a dozen chairs.

We made ourselves scarce, freshening up as best we could and pulling on our least-worn clothes. When we returned, the room was bustling, with several guests removing thick coats and greeting each other. Inuit people have massive hands with fat fingers and thick-set bulky bodies – they need them for the cold – and they look quite intimidating.

The kitchen was occupied by a large Inuit lady, who seemed to be using every pan in the building. The smell of the cooking was incredible: deep, rich and hearty. I felt my saliva glands going into overdrive.

Roberto introduced us to everyone and I said we would sit separately.

'They have laid places at the table for you – you must come and join us or they will be offended.'

Very few of them spoke English, but we exchanged nods and smiles and Roberto eventually ushered us to seats at the table. I was sitting next to a big guy wearing an old Pink Floyd t-shirt.

'This is the local vicar,' said Roberto. 'I'm afraid he doesn't speak English.'

I did a double-take – he didn't look like any vicar I had ever seen before. I nodded and smiled at him, wondering what must it be like to be a priest in such a remote place.

On my left was another guy, who was dressed in a button-down white shirt and slacks.

'This is Kuupik,' said Roberto. 'He speaks some English.'

I introduced myself and we got chatting while we waited for the food. It turned out that Kuupik had flown in from Nuuk to visit some family friends with his wife and kids. He was a civil servant back in the capital, but he hailed from Ammassalik originally.

'I have not spoken English for two years,' he said, 'but I speak to you.'

His language was indeed rusty and conversation was a little difficult, but it was clear he was delighted to get the chance to speak English and he was fascinated by our journey and the helicopter.

The smells from the kitchen intensified and soon the food was brought out. I was gob-smacked. Roast beef and roast pork, with potatoes, vegetables and loads of gravy. I could have been sitting in an English pub about to tuck into a Sunday roast, but here I was in Greenland, a country with no native cows or pigs, being served a spectacular roast. I had been half-expecting some sort of traditional Inuit dish of seal or fish, but I was more than happy with this fare. The portion sizes were huge – a proper plate of food – and I wolfed it down. It was delicious; perfectly cooked. The vicar next to me was barely cutting the meat; just shoving slabs of it in.

The dinner was delicious and a little wine with

it would be perfect. I turned to Roberto? 'Can I buy another bottle of that lovely Italian wine?'

'Wine?' He looked a little unsure and I was worried I'd put my foot in it. I did not want to upset our wonderful hosts.

'No problem, don't worry,' I said.

Deadly silence. What had I done?

'They don't drink,' Roberto whispered.

'I didn't know.'

Roberto looked carefully around at our guests' faces, before saying, 'But I think it's OK.'

From my previous trip to nearby Kulusuk some years earlier, I remembered the place had a busy bar. With very little else to do in the evenings, drinking played a big part in people's social life. Kulusuk has an airport with a tarmac runway, built by the Americans as a strategic base against the Russians during the Cold War, and still maintained by the US military. Because of that, there is more hustle and bustle in the place, and it feels rougher. The mentality in Ammassalik was evidently very different. In this village, with its prettily painted houses, its supermarket and its post office, the vibe felt more civilised. This slower pace suited me much better.

Roberto slipped away to the kitchen and returned with a bottle of wine, which Martin and I shared. We offered it to everyone else, but no one took any. Alcohol seemed to be considered an evil thing here, which wasn't surprising, given the damage it has inflicted on Inuit communities in Alaska, Canada and Greenland. Apparently few people in Ammassalik ever touched it.

I raised a glass to Martin across the table. Aside from my small faux-pas, this was bliss: the meal, the wine, the interesting company. These were the moments that made a trip like this special – the unexpected, unplanned encounters with the local people, seeing their kindness and a small part of the way they live. The conversation was stilted and I felt very conscious of being an outsider, but I also felt very honoured just being there, having a lovely meal with a lovely bunch who had invited us in, even during Covid. I mused on how unhelpful and selfish we are in the West by comparison.

At one point, one of our Inuit dining companions made some reference to their queen. It took me a moment to realise they meant the Danish queen, Margrethe II, whom they regarded as their sovereign as much as someone in Copenhagen might. I found that quite amazing; it seemed a bit out of kilter. Margrethe and the rest of the Danish royal family felt very distant from this remote land.

As the evening wore on, the impact of the flying and the long days of concentration began to take their toll on me. I saw Martin smiling along as he engaged in a sort of conversation with his neighbours at the table, but my brain was drifting towards bed.

Dessert was served: a red berry crumble with custard. I devoured it, trying to keep pace with the vicar. Wow, could that man eat!

After that, Martin nodded to indicate that he too was fading fast, so we bade our new friends farewell, thanking them for the delicious meal, and for opening their get-together up to some random madmen who'd dropped in unannounced from the sky.

As we left the table, Roberto asked, 'What time are you going?'

'We're planning on having breakfast for about eight, if that's OK?' I said. 'Then we'll get down to the helicopter for nine.'

'I'll drive you down.'

'Thanks very much. That will be great.'

He shrugged and smiled. 'I'd like to see your machine.'

I could hear the chatter and laughter from the dinner continuing, with the distinct, forceful Greenland accents travelling through the lodge. I didn't mind in the slightest. I was tired enough to block out any outside noise and was asleep not long after my head hit the pillow.

15
FACING THE FOG

The following morning, Roberto gave us a lift in his 4x4 to the clearing where we had parked the helicopter. The car crunched over the snowy gravel, turning down the long road towards the sea. In the distance, I could see our machine, its white metal glinting in the early light.

'I've told you I'm a doctor, yes?' he said as we drove down the hill.

I nodded. He had mentioned it.

'I'm retired, actually. Fifteen years now. Seems a long time ago. I run the Red House here six months of the year.'

'What do you do the rest of the time?'

'Travel. That is what I love to do, and work at the same time, looking for people to come here, to do their research.'

'I suppose times must be tough for the Red House at the moment?'

'They are, and it will continue to be difficult. You're the first visitors I've had in months.'

'You should promote it more. It's a fantastic place!' said Martin.

'You're right. People aren't going to come here if they don't know about it. But people are not going to come here now, that is for sure. Like you say, it is very tough.'

'Things will improve,' I said. 'Covid will pass and the Red House will have visitors again.'

Roberto sighed.

'Yes, maybe you're right that the Red House will have visitors again.' He paused. 'But I won't be around to welcome them.'

'Really? Why's that?'

He spoke softly. 'I have cancer.'

I turned towards him. 'I'm so sorry to hear that.'

He shrugged. 'It's life, isn't it? I've been having treatment for several years. Sadly, there's nothing else they can do. I don't think I'll be here when the expeditions return.'

'I know from personal experience that cancer's an evil thing,' I said.

'Have you had it?"

'Yeah. Brain tumour.'

'When was that?'

'I was diagnosed in 2007.'

'And you had chemotherapy?'

'Five months of it. I was told I was clear after that. Then there was the agonising five-year wait. They say if it's going to come back, it will usually do so within that time.'

Roberto didn't say anything.

I understood part of what he must be going through. I was lucky enough to have had people around me, to support me and help me pull through. It seemed like Roberto was alone here, locked up in his Red House to see out his days. The longer the Covid crisis continued, the greater his chances of dying alone.

He kept his eyes on the road as we approached the helicopter, speaking in such a matter-of-fact way about cancer you'd think he was talking about the weather.

Me and our lovely host, Roberto, at the Red House exploration lodge

He parked and we got out of the car, shooing away the more adventurous goats who'd got close to the helicopter.

My head was spinning a little as we stood next to the car, looking at the helicopter and the open bay in the distance. The water seemed like flowing tinfoil – peaceful, quiet and completely indifferent to the problems of humankind.

It was a profoundly sad moment. There's something about seeing amazing places and meeting amazing people. You always tell yourself, yeah, I'll come back here and when I do I'll see all these great people again and explore a bit further. I'd been doing that for the whole trip, saying I'd return to visit Nuuk some day, and revisit Sisimiut and Ammassalik. You have this illusion in your own mind that you'll do it, but you probably never will. Still, that illusion is treasured; something worth holding onto, something you can own. When something takes that away from you, and you know you'll never do something again, see someone again, it's quite emotional. Knowing that I would probably never see this kind, silver-haired Italian who had welcomed us with open arms into his house, fed us and showed an interest in our lives, when cancer and Covid had isolated him from the outside world, was heart-wrenching.

The tide continued to turn, a small iceberg bobbing harmlessly far out in the bay. I wondered how Roberto would remember this scene – what different meaning it might have for him.

We'd been standing in silence. A goat bleated, bringing the three of us back to reality.

Roberto smiled. 'Could I perhaps sit in the helicopter?'

'Of course,' I said.

Our host made his way over to the helicopter, seeming older and frailer now. I opened the cockpit door and he climbed up with a grunt, sliding into the pilot's leather seat.

'This is very good, isn't it?'

'You like it?'

His face had lit up as he surveyed the instruments with a sense of respect. It had been clear from our conversations over the past two days that this was a highly intelligent man, but now I could really see the scientist in him. He looked over the controls with the eyes of someone used to taking in information and deciphering what it all meant. I could see he was piecing together what each lever, each control, each dial did, and how they all fitted into the overall machine.

'This is the power lever?'

'Yes, and this over here, the cyclic, controls the direction of travel.'

I talked him through the instrument panel and the years seemed to melt away from him. He became like an excited schoolkid, a glint in his eyes from his thirst for knowledge. Even in this closing chapter of his life, Roberto wanted to understand everything, compute everything. I respected that so much, and it was a pleasure to be able to share what I knew about helicopters with him that day.

Once he'd had his fill, he smiled. 'Thank you, Jules,' he said.

'I can take you up for a quick spin, if you'd like?'

I was conscious of how much fuel we had left, but felt we could spare a little for a man who'd done so much for us.

He shook his head. 'This is enough.'

I took a picture of Roberto sitting in the cockpit, then he lowered himself from the helicopter back onto the ground.

'I'll let you get on now,' he said.

I gave him a hug.

'Thank you so much for everything,' I said. 'You've been so welcoming and wonderful to meet.'

Roberto smiled and made his way back to the car. He turned it around, crunching on the gravel, and drove off back towards the Red House. I watched him go. It felt like losing an old friend, despite having only known him for a couple of days.

I took a deep breath and turned back to the helicopter to face the familiar problems of our trip: we were behind schedule and the weather wasn't great.

Martin was already in the co-pilot's seat, plugging

FACING THE FOG

in the equipment and getting things ready. He'd remained quiet when I was chatting with Roberto, sharing our cancer experiences.

I walked round the aircraft carrying out all the checks, got the gear loaded up and pulled myself into my dry suit. We were going to be flying over the freezing ocean again, from Greenland to Iceland, which meant the risks were high and the rubber suits an unfortunate necessity. I really hadn't missed the pinch of the tight seal around the neck and wrists; the suit pulled hairs from my arms and felt oddly claustrophobic.

We hadn't been able to refuel at Ammassalik, because of lack of facilities, so the top priority was to get fuel. That meant a short hop across the bay to Kulusuk, with its big American airstrip. From there, fully fuelled up, the plan was to take the shortest route to Iceland, crossing to that country's nearest airport, Isafjördur on the northwest coast. The crossing would take about four and a half hours – getting close to our fuel limit once again.

We lifted off, straight up into the air and out over the sea, where there was thick cloud. I had hoped to be able to see Kulusuk once we got into the air, but as we approached, it was absolutely covered in fog.

'Maybe if we approach from the east, from the sea?' Martin suggested.

'I'll try.'

Kulusuk airport is right on the coast, so big

commercial aircraft come in low over the sea, between the mountains on either side and straight on to the runway. I was hoping that I'd be able to skirt around the bank of fog and come in underneath it in the same direction. That way, I'd be able to see ahead and should come in straight along the runway too.

I headed out to the east side and started dropping. Visibility was practically nil, so it was an act of faith more than anything. With the instruments on the panel, I could see how far above sea level I was, but not much else. If there was anything else out there, we could be in trouble.

I dropped down to 100ft and the fog suddenly cleared. Instead, right ahead of us loomed a huge iceberg. I banked hard, pulling the cyclic to the right, and the helicopter obeyed with extreme precision. My heart was in my mouth as the runners below the cockpit cleared the edge of the iceberg by what felt like inches. We were near enough to see the intricate, reflective patterns in the iceberg – far too close for comfort.

A second iceberg, or perhaps another peak of the same one, rose out of the water ahead of us. I yanked the cyclic back towards the left to make sure we were able to clear this one too, pulling back to give us a little more height to pass over the damned thing. The fog enclosed us once more.

'Crikey,' I said. 'That was too bloody close.'

I noticed that Martin's knuckles were white as my

normally unflappable co-pilot gripped his chair.

'I guess we risk the fog,' he said, always practical.

We continued blind for 30 seconds before we popped back out above the fog bank hanging like a big fat pillow over Kulusuk airport. I checked the GPS and positioned the helicopter directly over the runway, away from the control tower.

'Can I take it in?' asked Martin.

'Be my guest.'

'I have control?'

'You have control.'

Once we were in position and Martin had obtained clearance from air traffic control, he started to descend slowly towards the ground, both of us hoping to hell that he didn't encounter anything solid, such as a control tower or fuelling truck, on the way.

We descended into the thick, pillowy cloud again. And at around 200ft, it suddenly cleared and I had a glorious view of the runway. We missed the control tower by about 50ft. Martin radioed the tower to ask directions to the fuel pumps.

We landed beside the pumps and I hopped out, masked up, to greet the guys who approached us.

'Could you fuel us? Right to the top, and both tanks.'

By now, I knew the drill. These guys would fill up the helicopter and I'd head up to the control tower to pay. Usually, the chat was about the weather, because it's so important to pilots, and this time was no different. The

Danish guy up there, who was posted in Kulusuk for several months, told me there was a dodgy band of fog hanging over the sea, then a clear area from 500ft up to about 1,000ft, with very thick fog above it.

It didn't sound great, but the weather hadn't really been kind to us for most of the trip, so I wasn't expecting much else. We would have to go the whole way between Greenland and Iceland, Kulusuk to Isafjördur, in this narrow band between the cloud layers.

The worry was that we might fly into that opening between the bands of fog only to have it close up around us. Not just in front, but also behind. Then we'd have only one option: try and drop under the cloud and hope there was a gap of a few hundred feet between the cloud and the sea which we could fly in, without hitting any icebergs projecting out of the sea. Since that was a hideous prospect, we just had to pray that the present corridor would stay open for the next four hours.

I had such little familiarity with the weather patterns in the Arctic that I didn't know if the cloud moved up and down a lot, as it tends to do in Europe. That 500ft might seem like an enormous gap, but when you're flying along at 140mph, you're moving very fast and it can close up very quickly.

In the UK, above land, the weather is easier to predict; I know the weather patterns – the fog, especially. If you look at the fog over hills, it tends to lift and then come down again. If anything goes seriously wrong, you can land. The owner of the field you put the helicopter down in may not be best pleased, but I find it's better to ask for forgiveness than permission when the other option is crashing.

If I were in the UK in those weather conditions, I'd still be unhappy about it. I'd likely not go.

And now here we were in the Arctic, and I was going to have to fly in this gap for four hours, just hoping that it would remain open. It was a big ask.

16
BETWEEN THE CLOUDS

To leave or not to leave. That was the question.

If we didn't go, we hadn't got anywhere to stay for the night. And what if the weather was still as bad the next day, and the one after, and the one after that? When would we ever depart? We had the added pressure of the engineers waiting for us in Iceland.

Steeling myself, because I knew the next four hours were going to be uncomfortable, I decided to go.

The trouble with this kind of flying is that you're on edge the whole time. The adrenalin is pumping and it's exhausting. You're thinking, right, if the cloud comes down I've got to drop under the sea mist; I hope I can stay clear of the sea – any icebergs – and navigate OK. You're also thinking the weather might close in, both in front of you and behind. Then you'll be in the middle of icy, horrible weather and all you can think about is crash-landing in the freezing-cold water. If you somehow survive the landing, but you don't get the life raft out in time and get into it, it'll be curtains. Not great. Not great at all. Still, there was really nothing for it but to try.

Fully refuelled, we took off. The cloud was 200ft above us but I knew I could punch up through it and at 500ft there would be clear blue skies. I just needed to focus on the instruments for about 30 seconds in a complete white-out and we'd be through. Sure enough, as I took off, we were immediately enveloped in white cloud. Concentrate, Jules, concentrate… Tick, tick, tick… Then, whoosh! We exploded up into the bright sunshine and blue skies above the cloud. Below was this single massive pillow of fog, stretching as far as the eye could see – no land, no sea, just clouds, and off in the far west, the blue-white polar ice cap glacier rising majestically out of them. It was magnificent, but I didn't want to have to do that sort of refuelling again in a hurry.

I hadn't been able to see nearly as much of Greenland as I would have liked, but it was a brilliant place. Wonderful landscapes with generous, welcoming people, whom I would never forget.

However, it's hard to be too sentimental when your concentration is utterly engrossed in flying a helicopter. I felt this really was the last dangerous leg. We still had to fly from Iceland to the Faroe Isles, from there to Scotland, and then down across England and on to Guernsey. But we were heading south now, and the weather would be improving all the time. The sea would be getting warmer, which meant our chances of survival, should things go wrong, increased the further south we went. I switched on the reserve fuel tank and started pumping the extra 66 US gallons into the main fuel tank. I needed this to work again, as it had from Canada to Greenland.

We were leaving a country with a population of less than 60,000 to travel to one with a population of 350,000. Our journey would take us across 750 miles of ocean, empty but for the odd iceberg. But weather patterns change dramatically at coastlines, and now that we were leaving Greenland behind, we suddenly had cloud above us as well as below, with about a 500ft gap. We were making good progress, but we seemed confined to this dangerous, narrow band for the duration.

It does weird things to your eyes, flying through a band of cloud like that for so long. It felt like I'd gone partially blind, with everything at the top and bottom of my vision hazy and milky white. When your concentration is so intently focused on that tiny bit of light on the horizon, everything else goes kind of strange.

Nevertheless, I started to relax a little. There were no alarms going off, no warning lights blinking at me; everything seemed to be going swimmingly, so to speak, although I definitely didn't fancy swimming. The band of cloud seemed to be holding, so it was just a case of making minute adjustments to the cyclic to keep us steady at 1,500ft.

I asked Martin to take the controls for a minute so that I could take the opportunity to have a cup of tea. I opened the thermos, poured a cup, and reached for a couple of jelly babies. It was important to keep the energy levels up, and those jelly babies did wonders.

After ten minutes I took over from Martin once more, and time seemed to fly by. I was piloting in an almost hypnotic state until the sound of my phone beeping broke my trance. As ever, my phone was the first instrument on board to alert us that we were nearing land. We were still 100 miles or so from Iceland, but we would later learn that they have the most magnificent phone system here. There are masts all along the coast and their signal goes way out to sea. It's phenomenal.

I looked at the message on my phone. It was from the Bell guys who had flown to Iceland to meet us and were waiting for us there. They were checking in on our progress, so I let them know we'd be arriving soon, then got back to the task of flying the machine.

All of a sudden, the bands of cloud that had so consistently been above and below us on our journey towards Isafjördur lifted and cleared. It was as if my faulty vision had suddenly been fixed. We were treated to a glorious view of Iceland's coast, the cliffs leaping from the lively ocean in a dramatic fashion. The deep dark greens of the mountains and blues of the sky looked stunning in the mid-morning sun.

Isafjördur is remote, in the far northwest of Iceland, and our final destination was Reykjavik on the southwest coast, so we still had some way to go, but we desperately needed fuel. Isafjördur sits on a beautiful, expansive natural harbour. From our vantage point, we could see that the town was made up of neat rows of brightly coloured houses located on an L-shaped spit of land that reached out into the fjord. They were all dwarfed into insignificance by the mountain rising steeply behind them.

I called local air traffic control and was granted permission to land, flying over the town and across the water to reach the airport to the southeast.

I'd been to Iceland before, but nowhere anything like this remote corner. I gathered my face mask and gloves, got out of the helicopter and stretched. We had considered cracking on and flying direct to Reykjavik, but I doubted we had enough fuel and I was dying for a pee. If we'd gone straight to Reykjavik, which was another two hours of flying, I probably would have burst my bladder.

The guys fuelled us up while I took a quick comfort break and paid air traffic control. As I did so, I got a text from the Bell guys, checking on our ETA.

'When will you be in Reykjavik? We've got a nice

dinner lined up for you tonight.'

That would normally sound great, but I was already tired and I just wanted to get that helicopter to Reykjavik and then get my head down for a good night's sleep. The beauty of the fjords, the magnificence of the mountains, the simple brilliance of Isafjördur – none of that was as enticing as the prospect of a good bed and a decent rest.

With the helicopter fully fuelled, we took off again and headed south, leaving Isafjördur to fade into memory. As ever on this trip, I mused sadly that I would probably never get the chance to visit it again.

The weather for the flight south to Reykjavik wasn't good. The cloud had come in towards the coast. This was a great shame, as I knew the west coast of Iceland to be particularly striking. We had to look at it through a haze of fog: just imposing outlines of coast, cliffs and mountains as we flew overhead.

The first task was to fly over the huge peninsula next to Isafjördur. We crossed it uneventfully, enjoying the stunning landscape of the mountains and the black volcanic ash, then made the hop across the large, shallow Breidafjördur bay. With the cloud, I could stay low over the water, so this was an easy 30 minutes of flying.

I then had another peninsula to clear before Reykjavik, namely the Snaefellsjökull National Park. The Garmin computer system that gave me an indication of the height of the land ahead started warning me that I was too low. On the current trajectory I would hit the hills, and there were clouds above. I checked the map on my iPad. It showed a town ahead on the peninsula, with a mountain range behind. The town was called Grundarfjördur. I love these Viking names, and wondered about the original settlers in these remote locations – it must have been an incredibly hard life.

'What do you think?' I asked Martin. 'Over or around?'

The trouble was, with the low-lying cloud, we weren't entirely sure whether we'd be able to fly over the peninsula without getting pushed into the clouds. However, going around it would involve a huge loop, adding considerably to our time to Reykjavik.

'There's not a whole lot of room if we go over,' said Martin.

I could tell he was tired. By this time, I was utterly knackered too. I'd done an awful lot of flying that day – nearing seven hours. Both hands, both feet constantly in action. Small, tiny movements, little jiggles of the cyclic – doing that for the entire time. We'd both had enough. We just wanted some food and sleep.

I made the decision for both of us. 'We'll go over.'

As I neared the peninsula, I could see the town below, and through the fog I could make out the shape of the lighthouse on the coast. It felt very close beneath me. In reality, there was a good distance between us and the land, but helicopters have a strange way of making distance seem inconsequential. It felt as if our skids might hit a roof at any moment.

To my great relief, we cleared the town and carried on over the hills beyond. I headed for the col – the dip between mountain peaks in a summit line – between them; it felt as though the skids were kissing this col as we shot over it. I just managed to sneak over the top, and now we headed down the far side. It was iffy, but it saved a bucket-load of time and did wonders for our joint morale.

Some while afterwards, we passed the beautiful town of Akranes on our left and then Reykjavik came into full view. The fog was still present, but I could see the city – much larger than anything I had seen since southern Canada – with its rows of colourful-roofed buildings. I hadn't seen this many two-storey buildings in days, so it was a little bit of a shock. Even through the cloud, the imposing cathedral was visible on the horizon.

I radioed Reykjavik Airport, received clearance and then dropped straight down towards the runway.

The guys from the Bell team were waiting for us. They had a bright orange tractor with a tiny trolley behind it ready for the helicopter, on which I was expected to land. I always felt a little nervous landing the aircraft on such a small target, especially with the experts hanging around watching, but I managed to set down pretty much square on the trolley without a hitch. I jumped out and waved at the guys.

Andy Watts, the engineer, and Callum Hutchison, the support manager, were the UK representatives of Bell, and they were there to make sure everything was going well with the helicopter, and to carry out the 25-hour service. There was also the team from the local helicopter business, who were hosting us for the trip.

The tractor started up and towed the helicopter into the hangar for the maintenance work while we were greeted by the team.

'You guys must be exhausted,' said Andy. 'Let's get you to the hotel. Then you can take it easy.'

We must have looked like walking wounded. I wasn't exactly with it.

'Perfect,' I said.

I entered the hangar and peeled off the dry suit. It had started to feel overwhelmingly close, cutting off blood supply. Combined with my tiredness it was really frustrating me, and it was a huge relief to get it off. I stuck the dry suit on the seat of the helicopter, grabbed my bags, and Martin and I made our way out of the back of the hangar.

There was no passport control; we could apparently forget all that stuff. We walked into the car park, jumped into somebody's car and headed to the hotel. That was impressive – sort of super VIP.

We'd been booked into a hotel just on the outskirts

of Reykjavik, which was great. The places we'd stayed in so far had all been lovely but they were all very basic wooden shacks, and I was looking forward to a proper bed I could fit into, and a hot shower.

'Let's meet in the lobby at 7.30 – have a drink in the bar before we head out for dinner,' said Callum.

I'd completely forgotten about that. 'We're heading out for dinner?'

I felt like I had just run two marathons. But I knew Andy and Callum and the helicopter guys hosting us were making a huge effort to welcome me, and I didn't want to disappoint them,

'All the guys from the helicopter operation here are coming. They're really excited, as yours is the first Bell 505 ever to land in Iceland. They've arranged a few viewings for their interested clients tomorrow before you depart.'

I tried to appear delighted. I just hoped a good stiff drink would wake me up.

A little while later, revived by a hot shower, and wearing my one presentable outfit, I ventured out for the evening's entertainment, hoping I would manage to stay awake for the first hour at least, and feeling a little envious of Martin, who was remaining at the hotel for the evening, and would probably get a good rest.

When we arrived at the restaurant, a short-haired man in a blazer stood up and beamed at us.

'Hello Jules,' he said, arms open. 'I'm Ole Petter Bakken. It is a pleasure to meet you.'

Ole was the president and CEO of the Norwegian Aviation and Defence Group and he was hosting us for the meal. He covered Scandinavia and Iceland, and had flown out specially to meet us in Reykjavik. Part of his job involved selling helicopters in Norway – to the government, to commercial organisations and privately. Norway relies heavily on helicopters for search and rescue operations as well as tourism, and he said he was excited to meet me because my flight had proved just what the Bell 505 was capable of. I was the first person ever to fly a Bell 505 to Iceland and Greenland, and the fact that I'd also actually managed to fly it (almost) across the Atlantic, proved that it was

Out for dinner with the Bell reps, Ole Petter Bakken and the Icelandic guys

suitable for use in these extreme conditions, and thus Norway's conditions too.

From my perspective, the 505 could basically do everything the older Bell 407 could do. Also, it's a third of the cost to buy and requires less maintenance. I could understand why Ole was so interested in my trip.

He introduced us to his son, who was seated next to him. He was a handsome young man of around twenty, wearing a very trendy silver puffer jacket with a big black fur collar. He maybe wasn't quite as excited to meet us as his father, but I learned later that he was trying to kick off a modelling career, and I wished him the best of luck.

Ole was a larger-than-life, ex-military guy who was full of energy. He positioned himself directly opposite me at the table and made sure the drinks were flowing.

'Jules,' he boomed, 'what do you want to drink?'

'Wine would be great,' I said.

'Of course.' He signalled impatiently to a waiter. 'Let's get wine for everybody.'

I was very glad he had been kind enough to host the evening. Food and drink are phenomenally expensive in Iceland, and we were in a fancy restaurant in the capital so I dreaded to think what the evening's dinner was going to cost.

The wine arrived, the meal was delicious and the evening flowed. He asked me what drove me to attempt such crazy feats as this trip and my Everest climb, and listened with fascination when I talked about them. He generously presented me with a number of Bell souvenirs, including a pin-badge of which only five had been made. Reynir Petursson, a Viking-like helicopter pilot, made a late-night video-phone call to a UK helicopter engineer, Dave Knight, whom he and I both knew. Dave had been very sceptical about the viability of my journey, particularly given how new the helicopter design was. It was gratifying to hear him admit that it was after all possible and congratulate me on my achievement thus far. After that, I could keep my eyes open no longer.

I thanked Ole and everyone else for their great hospitality and made my way back to the hotel, where I crawled into bed.

The following evening, after the helicopter's service had been completed, we would leave Reykjavik and fly to the fishing town of Höfn on the southeastern coast of Iceland. I had nothing to do until then, so I could chill out for the day. Or so I thought.

17
FLYING ON FILM

Martin was feeling rough after staying up drinking until the early hours with some people he'd met in the hotel bar. I decided to take a look around the centre of Reykjavik and meet him at the airport around 5pm for our evening flight to Höfn, whose own small airport was Iceland's closest to the Faroe Isles. Our plan was to refuel there and minimise the length of the flight over the ocean.

Reykjavik is a wonderful city. It reminds me a bit of Holland – that sort of architecture. I wandered aimlessly through the streets.

After checking out the maritime museum, Perlan, and the natural history museum, which is housed in a glass dome resting on six water tanks, I took a stroll to the old harbour. It's the main port of departure for whale- and puffin-watching tours, as well as Northern Lights cruises. I wanted to find some presents for

Steph and Liz. I had been missing the girls a great deal and at times, especially during the crossing from Canada to Greenland, I had feared I might never see them again. The thought was unbearable.

The whole of the city is heated for free by the hot volcanic springs underneath Iceland. The hot water is pumped through a huge pipe into the city and around all the buildings. It's absolutely amazing and really intrigues the engineer in me.

As I was wandering around the Kringlan shopping mall in the middle of the afternoon, I received a call from Callum, Bell's support manager in the UK. He sounded flustered.

'Can you get back to the airport for four o'clock?'

I checked my watch.

'I can, but we're not due to be there until five, to get ready and leave at six.'

I was concerned that there might be a problem with the helicopter. The idea of losing another day was not good. I was really hoping to be able to spend the weekend with my daughters.

'Yeah, but we've had a call from Iceland's 10 o'clock news programme. They want to interview you.'

'What? TV?'

'They're down at the hangar now.'

I rushed back to the hotel to pick up my things. I was still a little bit jaded from the day before, I hadn't packed and now I had to get myself mentally prepared to be interviewed by a TV reporter, all on top of my nerves about departing. The adrenaline was pumping by the time I reached the hotel.

I arrived at the airport just before four and was greeted by Callum, who took me to meet the news crew. There were just two of them – a reporter and a cameraman. The presenter was a stunning blonde with piercing eyes – very distracting, and not good when you're being interviewed.

She launched straight into prep mode for the interview. 'I'd like to interview you about your expedition,' she said.

'No problem,' I said.

'I hear you've climbed Everest and this is your next challenge. I'll ask you about the trip, the problems you've faced and where you're going next. Is that OK?'

'Sure. Do you want me to put the dry suit on before you interview me?'

I pointed out my dry suit. I didn't actually have to wear it for the next leg, as we were mostly flying over land, but I thought it might look more professional on camera.

'A good idea.'

She was very matter-of-fact and to the point. I don't know what I was really expecting, but I remembered that when I went on BBC Breakfast to promote my book *Aftershock*, about my experiences on Everest, I had to go to make-up before the interview. There was certainly none of that here. It was just me, in my dry suit, in the hangar, with the helicopter in the background.

The camera started rolling and I felt like a deer in headlights. The reporter asked about the trip so far and where we were heading next. I gave her a brief summary.

'Is it scary?' she asked.

'You could say that.'

'Why?'

'There's no de-icing, there's no special equipment on this helicopter – it's just me, my co-pilot and the elements. It's a long way up, and it's very cold.

'And why are you doing the trip?'

'The helicopter needed bringing back so I had the crazy idea to fly it – and it's a lot of fun,' I said. 'It's also for a good cause as well.'

'What is that?'

'A haemotology cancer-care charity in London.' I pointed to the scar on the side of my head. 'I've had cancer.'

'And what about Everest? I hear you've climbed it.'

'That was back in 2015. I was there when the avalanche happened in Nepal, and I was nearly buried alive.'

Just when I felt I was getting into the swing of things, the interview was over. The news presenter thanked me and started packing away her microphone. That

FLYING ON FILM

Waving to the news crew before departing Reykjavik

must be it, I thought. Now I can get back to prepping for the flight and focusing on the next leg to Höfn.

But then Reynir Petursson, the chief helicopter pilot whom I had met at the dinner the previous night, came over and said, 'Hey, Jules, by the way, we're going to follow you out of Reykjavik airport in our Bell 407 and film you departing and heading off.'

'You are?' I must have looked shocked.

He laughed. 'We're going to fly next to you and film you as you're flying. A bit like *Mission Impossible*. You know – Tom Cruise!'

That really did get the juices flowing.

'How are we going to do this?' I said.

'You take off, you get to 80 knots, I'll take off with

the TV cameraman with me, and we'll be on your left-hand side. Stick to 80 knots and you'll be fine. Oh, and whatever you do, don't bank left. You can bank right, but don't bank left because you'll hit us.'

The way he said this made me incredibly nervous.

'How's the weather looking out there?' I asked.

'It's minimal,' he said, meaning the fog was the lowest you can fly in. 'But you'll be OK – you're a good pilot; you've flown all this way and you haven't killed yourself so far. Cloud level is down to around 100ft over the sea.'

'So, it's that grim?'

'You'll get to Höfn, though.'

My rule is never to rush when you're flying. But I was now about to break it: there was pressure to do this filming and suddenly we were all rushing for the film crew.

We prepped everything for take-off, checking the helicopter over, and sooner than I would have liked, it was time to roll.

I was at the controls, Martin to my left. There was a row of people standing outside the hangar, watching the take-off with interest. I saw Reynir give a thumbs-up. It's just like every other take-off, I told myself. Only everybody is watching, and if you crash now they're going to have it on tape.

I lifted off from the trailer and hung in a hover. I could see the cameraman filming us as we rose steadily. I turned towards the south and slowly moved off. Normally, I'd crack on, but I had to wait for the 407, so I hung awkwardly near the edge of the airfield.

'Head for the pass directly ahead.' Reynir's voice crackled through my headset. He sounded a million miles away when he was just metres from us.

The fog had come right down now and I couldn't see the pass he was talking about. In fact, the fog was so low that I was on the verge of turning back. I could tell by the look on Martin's face that he was having second thoughts too.

'Through the pass?' I said.

'Yeah, you can see the road below,' said Reynir. 'You follow the road straight up to the pass, and then you're through and down the other side. Follow the car going up the pass. Park on its roof.'

I took it that he wasn't speaking literally.

I could see the road below – he was right – but not that clearly. It was a slightly darker vein through a sea of grey. I also saw the car. I descended so that I was above the vehicle and started following it up the pass. We were heading directly south out of Reykjavik, which meant we were heading towards a massive peninsula with the international airport on its tip.

Our plan was to head straight down over this peninsula, towards a town called Porlakshöfn. Then we would drop straight down to the sea on the other side and crawl along the coast to get to Höfn. It all sounded great in theory – which is often the case – but the cloud and the fog were very low, so there was no chance of flying slightly inland and enjoying the view, as we'd hoped. In that fog, there was no view.

Still, Höfn airport was on the coast, which meant we should still be able to see it when we came in to land. There was another international airport further inland, which we had originally intended to head towards, but because the land rises so steeply from the coast, we knew it would be completely covered in fog.

The whiteout was unremitting, even on the coast, and I was very conscious of the fact that I had this red 407 just off to the left of me, trying to get as close as possible to get good film footage in the awful, foggy weather.

Don't bank left, don't bank left, I repeated to myself as I maintained altitude and speed, following the thin grey line.

'Bloody hell,' I muttered into the microphone.

Martin twisted in his seat, trying to get sight of the trailing 407. It was nowhere to be seen.

A crackle, and the voice returned.

'Over the col. Follow the road,' it said.

By this stage I really was practically parked on the car roof. Goodness knows what the driver thought – perhaps people in Iceland are used to this.

The col nearly caught me unawares. The land rose up and the fog held still, meaning the gap was closing up. We mustn't go into the thick fog. I breathed in as we just cleared the col. There was movement below us – a flash of colour in the grey. There was the car again, trundling along the road below us, dropping down from the summit line.

'This is nuts,' I said.

The voice over my headset stayed calm.

'OK, Jules, to the right, gently. Follow the road, follow the road.'

I banked right, headed down over the far side of the col.

'Is he there?' I asked Martin, who was still peering out of the window.

'Christ, he's right there,' he confirmed. 'He's almost touching us.'

These Icelandic pilots are nuts; Reynir was in my blind spot to the left, so close it felt like the blades were touching.

'Bank left – tight left now,' he instructed. 'I will fly over you.'

'Did he say bank left?' Martin said.

'I think so.'

Don't bank left, don't bank left; that was all that had been going through my mind. He'd specifically told me not to bank left when we were safely on solid ground, now he wants to bank left and he's going to fly over me?

'Turning tight left now,' I said to Reynir.

I banked left, praying I wouldn't feel a crunch of blades. There was a whoosh of air, the beat of blades just above as the 407 nipped over to the other side of me. They re-adjusted, further out to sea than us now, and matched our speed and altitude.

'That was good; the film crew are happy. I want you to fly along the cliffs now,' I heard Reynir say.

The white cliffs had risen to our left, along the coast. I dropped below them and the 407 followed. I kept my concentration dead ahead, but in my peripheral vision, I could now see the red helicopter.

I shot a quick glance at it and could see the back doors open, the cameraman pointing the camera straight at us. This was seriously crazy stuff.

'Fantastic,' said Reynir. 'That's perfect. We're done. See you guys. Safe flight.'

And with that, the red speck in the corner of my eye banked to the right and within seconds it was gone.

We were alone again. I looked at Martin and we both broke into laughter.

'Jesus, let's not do that again,' he said.

I rose up again, lifting clear of the white cliffs to give us some breathing room. The adrenaline was pumping; that was crazy fun. That was my overall impression of Icelandic people from this trip: crazy fun. They're a great bunch, even if they do make you think you're going to die in a heap of twisted metal in the middle of nowhere. It's funny but there was a great sense of

FLYING ON FILM

On Iceland's evening news!

comfort with Reynir – he might be crazy but he was a very experienced pilot and knew this area like the back of his hand. I felt that as long as I followed his instructions to the letter I would be safe. Now that he was gone, and we were back out to sea, it felt lonely – just us in our little glass bubble.

We continued to follow the coast. The weather was absolutely awful. To the left we passed two huge glaciers that flowed straight down into the sea. I couldn't resist flying in to take a closer look at one. The dirty white ice seemed completely immovable, but I knew there were huge forces pushing this lump inexorably towards the ocean.

There was a loud crack, a boom like dynamite going off. A huge chunk of the glacier near the water's edge suddenly broke free and went crashing down into the water, erupting the calm ocean into frenzied motion. It was very humbling to be able to see such a fantastic natural landscape from our unique vantage point.

Soon, however, we had to tear ourselves away, conscious of our fuel; the helicopter acrobatics with the film crew had already burned off more than planned.

The fog continued to descend; the weather really was minimal, to use Reynir's expression. I didn't dare go inland. I continued to hug the coast, about 50ft off the sea, so that if the fog continued to come right down I could put the helicopter down on the sandy shoreline.

It wasn't an ideal way to fly, but we felt it was the best way to stay safe, with an effective exit strategy if things went awry. We ended up flying like that for two hours, before we started our approach to Höfn.

Höfn knew we were coming in, as we'd phoned the control tower before we left Reykjavik. The airport was literally one guy in a tiny two-storey control tower. It was nearing 8.30pm when I radioed to let him know we were near.

Once he'd granted us clearance, I asked if there was anywhere we could stay. We had no accommodation sorted in Höfn and it was clearly a tiny place – basically a very remote farming hamlet.

'My friend has a farmhouse here. They usually have accommodation. I will give her a call for you and let you know.'

'Brilliant,' I replied. 'And is there anywhere to get some food?'

'You can eat at the farmhouse.'

'Can you call a taxi for us?'

'There are no taxis here, but I'll give you a lift.'

Where in the world do you find the air traffic controller giving you a lift to your hotel? These Icelandic people really are great.

Another crackle and he was back on the radio.

'Yes, I've booked everything for you,' he said. 'You must rush though, because they finish serving at nine.'

We were going as fast as we could, but the idea of missing food gave us an extra push. Never rush? True, but that also depends on what time the dining room closes.

We came blasting in to Höfn airport, landing the helicopter by the fuel tank. A small, well-built man, standing there in pouring rain, was waiting to meet us.

'Get in,' he said, motioning towards his car. 'I've arranged for you to be fuelled up. I'll take you to the farmhouse.'

Unbelievable – chauffeur service!

We grabbed our stuff from the helicopter and jumped into the car, with our driver/controller tearing out of the airport as if getting us to the farmhouse in time for dinner was a matter of life and death.

'What time do you want to leave tomorrow?' he asked as he navigated the rain-soaked roads.

'About 8 o'clock,' I said.

'I'll pick you up from the farmhouse at 7:30, then I'll open the airport.'

I was gobsmacked. He was opening up the airport – his little airport – to accommodate us. It was a proper airport, of course, with a tiny control tower, a fire engine and everything, but there was just this one guy running it, and he was really going out of his way to help us. Top chap.

The car pulled up in front of a long, wooden building that I assumed must be the farmhouse. It was a quarter to nine, so we rushed straight into what looked like the restaurant and spoke to one of the waitresses.

'We'd like something to eat, please, if possible,' I said. 'We don't need to check into the rooms yet; we're happy to eat first.'

'Follow me,' she said.

Once we were seated at a table, we had a look through the menu and the waitress returned to take our orders.

'What's this thing?' I asked, pointing at a dish I didn't recognise.

'It's Harofiskur, our speciality – dried fish. It's very good.'

'OK, I'll try that for starters.'

Soon, a dish was served with thin strips of dried fish sticking out of the top of a glass with some butter placed in the centre. There was no way to cut it, so I picked it up and tore off a chunk with my teeth. It was like chewing a bit of old leather.

With a smile, the waitress said, 'You have to chew it

slowly and it will melt in your mouth!'

I slapped on some of the butter and took another bite. I was chewing and chewing and chewing, and with my saliva and the butter softening up the fish, the flavours really started to come through. It had a pleasing texture to it now, and I ended up thoroughly enjoying it. I do like to try the local dishes when I travel to foreign places – more often than not they are a real surprise and delight. But for my main, I had spaghetti. I needed to make sure I got some actual sustenance and carbs.

Once we'd finished, we checked in properly and went to our rooms. I was about to hit the sack when my phone started buzzing – a number I didn't recognise. I answered.

'Is this Jules?' asked a voice.

'It is.'

'I am from Höfn airport. I forgot to say, you cannot fly tomorrow.'

'You're kidding me?'

'We are not an international airport; you don't have clearance for tomorrow.'

I could barely keep my eyes open, but having another day wasted with no flying was not going to be good. Simply not an option.

I spent the next few hours with Martin, frantically trying to get clearance. We filed flight plans, sent emails, made calls – everything we could think of to sort this out. We tried to explain that we'd come to Höfn because it was a shorter distance from there to the Faroe Isles and also because of the fog.

In the end, we were told that they'd try to sort it out by the morning. I went to bed fearing the worst.

18
SUNSHINE IN THE FAROE ISLES

The guys at air traffic control were as good as their word. We were cleared to take off for the Faroe Isles. A customs officer would meet us at the airport in order to complete all the checks and forms.

We left the farmhouse to find the airport owner waiting for us in his car, grinning wildly. 'You're lucky,' he said. 'They don't do this very often.'

He whizzed us back to the airport, where we met the customs official and signed all the forms. I pulled the collective lever and we lifted up into the cold morning air.

I'd crossed Canada, found remote airfields and managed to stay fuelled up. I'd navigated the crossing to Greenland, avoiding the killer clouds and somehow kept the helicopter going despite all the warning alarms. On top of that, I'd landed on the polar ice cap, stayed in remote villages and managed another perilous ocean crossing to Iceland. Now we were over the sea once again, but with every passing mile we were getting closer to UK airspace and the final leg of our journey. I felt more confident now that we'd be within rescue distance if something went terribly wrong.

The weather was far nicer than we'd experienced for quite some days. The cloud cover was minimal, the sun was out and we had great visibility ahead of us, the deep blue ocean rolling along below like a vast soft carpet. Things really seemed to be looking up as we started to head south towards the Faroe Isles. I was acutely aware of the forecast that said the elements were due to take a bit of a turn later that afternoon, but I was keeping that out of my mind and really enjoying the moment.

The flight to the Faroe Isles only took a couple of hours; before long we could see land on the horizon. The islands seemed so isolated and remote. From our bird's-eye vantage point, we could see all eighteen of them, with the largest, Streymoy, dwarfing the rest. Lush green cliffs marked the coasts, with gushing waterfalls here and there. The majority of the islands seemed totally devoid of life – just massive lumps of rock sticking out of the sea with no buildings on them.

As I closed in on the airport, I could make out several settlements on the main island, their windows

SUNSHINE IN THE FAROE ISLES

catching the light.

By now I was suffering from a familiar problem: I was bursting to go to the toilet. Having overdone the tea from my flask on the flight over from Iceland, I was paying the price. I had been enjoying the flight in the sunshine so much, I almost didn't want it to end, but at the same time my bladder was in a desperate state.

Vagar airport was in a spectacular fjord location, with the runway ending right on the water's edge. Planes come into the fjord, with its steep-sided mountains, flying low over the sea and straight onto the runway. It would be quite dramatic to land here in a plane. In the helicopter, you can just stop dead and pop it down. Not recommended – they call this dead man's curve – but it's possible. You should really come in at 60 knots (roughly 70 mph) in case of engine failure. Basically, if the engine fails and you're high up and stationary, the helicopter will drop like a stone. If you're flying at 60 knots and the engine stalls, with the forward momentum the wind will keep flowing through the blades and you can fly the helicopter to the ground. It will be a bumpy landing but at least you've got a chance. Remember the Leicester City football club owner's helicopter flight out of the stadium – straight up? When a bearing failed in the tail rotor, the aircraft spun out of control then dropped straight down again. That's a horrific example of dead man's curve.

I radioed the tower and soon we were on solid

ground again. I removed my headset, put on my mask and gloves and climbed down from the cockpit. Behind me, a large Scandinavian Airlines jet touched down on the runway. I stood watching it come to a halt and taxi towards arrivals. I was staggered by the sheer size of the thing compared with our tiny little glass bubble. It astounded me that Bell could build this helicopter at a fraction of the cost of that enormous plane and it could do pretty much the same thing. Incredible engineering.

A ground team approached in a truck and I asked them to fuel us right up.

'Sure thing,' the main guy said. 'You'll need to go through to the back office to pay.'

No problem, I thought. By now I was fairly used to navigating the back areas of airports. It was always the same and we usually ended up in the control tower, forking out whatever fee they'd decided on that day.

I took Martin's passport, leaving him with the helicopter, crossed towards the door the ground crew had indicated and spoke with the man inside. He was a gruff, no-nonsense sort of guy.

Once I'd paid for the fuel, he sprang an extra surprise.

'There's also a $500 entry fee,' he said.

'Entry fee? We've never had to pay an entry fee before.'

'That's our standard charge for processing you here. You can either pay the entry fee here, or you can go and queue through customs with everyone else.'

SUNSHINE IN THE FAROE ISLES

I was shocked. Five hundred dollars to look at a passport!

'I'll go through customs with everybody else,' I said.

I left without another word and skirted the edge of the airport towards the main arrivals gate.

I ended up getting folded in with the passengers disembarking from the Scandinavian Airlines jet. I got quite a lot of stares, which was disconcerting until I remembered I was still dressed head-to-toe in my bright-orange dry suit. I looked like an astronaut.

I queued for around fifteen minutes before filling in two forms and handing the passports over to one of the border staff. He didn't bat an eyelid at my unusual attire, didn't ask a single question about Covid compliance. A quick look at the passports and I was through – and $500 better off.

By now, my bladder really was close to bursting. I made straight for the nearest loo, and wrestled with my rubber suit – just in time. The relief was enormous. At last, I now felt I could enjoy the next leg of the flight to Scotland.

I was sorry not to be staying overnight in the Faroe Isles – they looked magical. I wondered who visits this enchanting-looking place. Hardly anyone nowadays, I imagined, because planes don't need to refuel there: they go on to Iceland. But I had arranged to pick up my daughters the following day, so I had to crack on. Another time, I hope.

ARCTIC INSANITY

Normally there is an awful lot of fog on the Faroe Isles, but that day there was only a thin mist and the weather was holding. Which meant we had to make the most of it for flying, and get to Scotland before the forecast bad weather started to close in.

With customs cleared and fuel paid, I headed back to the helicopter, which the ground team had just finished refuelling. We climbed in, I called the tower for clearance and we rose upwards into the glorious sunshine, then out over the deep blue sea, across the fjord.

With their impressive cliff faces and bright green surfaces, the islands looked like something out of *Avatar* – with more lush vegetation than anywhere else

Faroe Isles – I wish I'd had longer here

SUNSHINE IN THE FAROE ISLES

I had ever seen. And many of those islands were uninhabited – what a great place to explore.

We flew out over the open ocean, finally on our way to Scotland. I was excited: arriving on UK soil would mean I had achieved the objective of being the first person to fly a Bell 505 across the Atlantic. But I didn't want to count my chickens, as I still had 220 nautical miles of sea to cross. At normal cruising speed, that would take more than two hours – no negligible feat in this tiny glass bubble.

I had my sights set on Stornoway, on Lewis, the most northerly island of the Outer Hebrides, for a refuel stop. By now I had a strong tailwind and we were ripping along at close to 200 mph across the ocean surface – a genuine thrill. These are the flying days a pilot dreams of, when the sun is shining and the sky is blue. I was living the dream.

'You getting hot?' asked Martin.

'Yeah, and some numpty broke the heating controls,' I said, laughing.

I had been trying to treat the warm weather as a nice change, but the beating sun on the Perspex bubble of the helicopter was really starting to warm up the cockpit – particularly given that we were both still wearing our dry suits, which were made of 2mm-thick rubber with an additional orange cloth on the outside. Of course, when you're flying, you have to keep the suit zipped up around your neck with the sleeves all fastened up, because there wouldn't be time to start zipping and fastening things if you suddenly found yourself heading for the sea. Your neck is sealed, your arms are sealed and your feet are in little waterproof booties, with your shoes on top of these. I know people who would love this heat. But I was getting very warm and sticky.

We were hot and I was also dying for the toilet again, because, idiotically, I just kept drinking the tea from my flask. I was caught between having the most elating experience of my life – flying in fabulous sunshine towards Scotland; spotting the Highlands on the horizon; the sense of freedom as we flew – and at the same time, really wanting to rip that damn suit off and take a leak.

Finally the Isle of Lewis came into view. I could see the light blue ocean, clear as glass, spreading out in front of us, and in the distance, the greeny-yellow coastline of Lewis. The helicopter basked in the brightest sunlight of our trip and, even with my peaked cap and aviator sunglasses, I was squinting to see properly. We had made it, and it felt like the weather gods were welcoming us to Scotland.

I radioed the tower as we caught our first sight of Stornoway. The airport was fairly basic – a strip of tarmac surrounded by a load of grass, stuck on a headland. There was really nothing else there, apart from what I'd heard was a fairly sophisticated control

SUNSHINE IN THE FAROE ISLES

tower. I called again, got clearance and then came into land. After putting the helicopter down, I looked at Martin, gave him a nod and shook his hand; the worst was surely behind us.

I opened the door, gasping for air, and swung myself out of the helicopter. I tugged violently at the neck and wrist straps of the dry suit as I ripped it off and collapsed onto the ground. A cool breeze slid up the runway and washed over me. Bliss! I lay spread-eagled on the tarmac, looking up at the blue sky, the blades of the helicopter glinting above me. I let out a whoop of joy as I lay there. I wasn't sure if I'd ever move again, but I didn't care. The magnitude of the trip and what I'd achieved was starting to sink in.

But I still had to finish the job. My final destination,

Collapsing on the ground at Stornoway – I had done it!

Guernsey, was still hundreds of miles south, so we needed to fuel up and get cracking.

I hurried over to the tower to pay, feeling completely liberated from the dry suit, while the ground team set about refuelling. I returned to the helicopter and radioed the tower for clearance to take off again, feeling more impressed than ever with the 505. She had kept going through the most incredibly tough legs of the journey.

The plan from Stornoway was to fly over the mountains of Scotland, including Ben Nevis, and land at Cumbernauld airfield, just to the east of Glasgow. Here I would part ways with Martin, who planned to grab a night's sleep and then catch a flight back to Ireland. My own plan was to fly on to my dad's place in Derbyshire for the night.

So there was still a lot of flying ahead of me.

19

A ROLLERCOASTER RIDE

I headed straight out over the Minch, the stretch of water separating the Outer Hebrides from mainland Scotland. The weather was starting to close in, with the sun obscured by thick clouds. I coasted in over Gairloch, heading into the mountains which stretched all the way from the Liathac range immediately in front of us, all the way to Ben Nevis which, at 4,413ft, is the UK's highest peak, and beyond.

The turbulence hit us almost as soon as we entered the mountains. The smooth flight over the ocean was a distant memory – and the rollercoaster ride from hell began. Bash, crash, bash as the helicopter was thrust from left to right, up and down, backwards and forwards. It took all my skills to keep her in the air.

Helicopters can take a certain amount of turbulence, but it says in the manual that this machine will not like sustained turbulence over a long period of time.

'There are a lot of mountains to cross,' I said to Martin. 'This is knocking nine bells out of us.'

'We could go around the coast?'

That was the choice we faced. The coastal option would add extra miles, and possibly require an additional refuelling stop; otherwise we could brave the turbulence and go over the mountains, enabling us to reach Cumbernauld in one go.

'We've had good luck tackling these things head on so far,' I said. 'So we could crack on. You reckon she'll hold together?'

'Let me have a go,' said Martin.

He took over the controls. Thirty seconds later he shouted, 'Christ, this is rough.'

'You see, it wasn't my dodgy flying.'

'I'm handing back over – you have control.'

'I have control,' I confirmed.

Bang bash crash, up and down, and from side to side we went. Every time I entered a valley we were batted around senselessly. When I cleared a ridge, we shot into the air on the updraft. It wasn't long before I was feeling seriously sick.

I thought back to Bell's famous Huey helicopter, which was used to transport troops into the Vietnam jungle. It was the first time helicopters had really been used in active combat. The Hueys took the severest punishment but survived. The Bell Jet Ranger was then developed from the Huey technology, becoming

A ROLLERCOASTER RIDE

Beautiful Scottish scenery on the way to Cumbernauld

statistically the safest aircraft in the world. The 505 was developed from the Jet Ranger. On that basis, the 505 should be able to survive a battlefield, so why not also the extreme turbulence of the Scottish Highlands? That's what I told myself as my head was smashed into the side window again—

'Ow, that bloody hurt!'

We carried on, as agreed, straight towards the mountains proper, and suddenly they were upon us. They'd gone from inconsequential bumps on the horizon to threatening, hulking land masses that dwarfed our tiny helicopter.

The uplift was enormous, shooting up from underneath and pulling us upwards as if we had been grabbed by one of those mechanical arms in an arcade claw game. I felt that I was just about in control of the machine, but at any moment, we knew, the turbulence could take over.

We cleared a ridge and shot up in the air, in what felt like a near-vertical uprush. Then we nose-dived back down again. Our stomachs seemed to take a while to come back down with us. The helicopter continued to be slammed from side to side and up and down. Out of the windscreen the view was becoming a blur and my eyes were starting to see double.

I maintained the same level of power while navigating this particularly aggressive turbulence, but rather than the blades pushing down the air to lift us up, the wind was pushing both the blades and the helicopter. It was a massive and overpowering force, shoving us upwards.

In commercial jets, small pockets of turbulence are a regular occurrence and people have come to expect them – everybody goes *woooaah* but you've got a smooth-talking captain over the tannoy to keep you feeling safe. This was nothing like that at all. It was violent and unpredictable; as if the elements were really out to get us; as if they were throwing everything they had at us to prevent us from crossing the mountain range and instead tried to pull our tiny glass bubble to pieces.

As the latest uprush subsided I pushed the lever forward, headed down again to get us back to a sensible altitude. Woah, man alive!

Of course, we were being buffeted around the top of the plateau. We'd spot a valley ahead of us and head straight for it. But as soon as we dropped down into it, the wind would bounce off both sides of the valley, throwing us from side to side. I really thought our machine would be broken into pieces. I tried to convince myself it could take it, but in the moment, with the bang, bang, boom of the wind smashing into the thin layer of protection the helicopter gave us, it felt totally hellish.

'Do you think it's going to be alright?' I shouted to Martin.

'Fucking hope so!'

We ran out of valley and hit the next mountain range, thrown up in the air once more by the wind. We were slammed and banged around, but somehow we stayed in one piece.

'Do you think we should turn back and try to go around this lot?' I said.

He was silent for a minute, clearly weighing up the options.

'I think we're here now.'

Too right. We bloody well were – and how I wished we weren't! With no other realistic option, we made the decision to go on and see how bad it could get. The mountains were getting bigger and bigger, higher and higher, but as they did so, the turbulence seemed to ease off a bit. That was a good sign, so I continued to seek out altitude wherever I could.

All the while I was feeling sicker and sicker. I'm usually fine and hadn't had any issues on our trip until now, but we were just being banged around so madly. So as well as not knowing how much the helicopter could take, I also didn't know how much more *I* could take.

'I can't believe it,' I said to Martin. 'We've done a bloody transatlantic flight in this thing and our epitaph is going to read 'They died over the mountains in Scotland'.'

We were trying to stay in the middle of the valleys wherever we could, flying high above them and the mountain tops, so that at least we weren't being buffeted in all directions at once. This carried on for about two hours. They were two of the most gruelling, stressful and nerve-racking hours of the trip – and that includes the crossing from Canada to Greenland when it seemed as if the entire machine was packing in and we were heading into the sea.

Finally, unbelievably battered and bruised, we broke clear of the mountains and found ourselves over relatively flat land, where the turbulence dropped and we were able to breathe again.

On the upside, Scotland is a beautiful country, and the mountains look especially magnificent from the sky. We had actually had some stunning aerial glimpses of

A ROLLERCOASTER RIDE

them. It was just a shame that we hadn't been in much of a mood to appreciate the view.

We headed for our next stop. Cumbernauld is a small airport. All the main flights come into the much larger Glasgow Airport, or to Edinburgh, so Cumbernauld was perfect for us: quieter, out of the way and cheaper.

I called the tower, received clearance and let the helicopter down onto the tarmac near the fuel pump. It seemed we were the only people dropping in that day, but we were used to that. A man came out, greeted us and got down to refuelling the helicopter. We had a good chat about the hazards of our transatlantic trip while he did so.

Martin took his bags from the helicopter and arranged for the fuel guy to give him a lift to his hotel. It was strange, knowing that I was going to be on my own for the rest of the trip. I have usually flown solo and in some ways I actually prefer it, but Martin had been indispensable on this trip – a safe pair of hands if I needed a short break for a cuppa from my flask, and an experienced sounding board about routes, weather conditions and a whole host of technical stuff that you need to be on top of during an expedition like this. He also knew that this was my challenge, that he was there for the ride, to help out where he could, but to allow me the space to make decisions, take control and do the majority of the flying. He was a perfect co-pilot and a great comfort blanket. I was sad to see him go.

'Cheers for everything, Martin,' I said, giving him a hug.

'It was one hell of a journey,' he grinned.

'You can say that again.'

'If you're thinking about any other mad helicopter expeditions, give me a shout.'

'Don't worry, I will.'

Throughout this trip, there had been no support team in the traditional sense. It was just me and a co-pilot I'd roped in to lend me a hand. We had no helpers on the ground booking hotels and other things every day. I'd heard about people who have done these sorts of adventurous, challenging trips and had twenty-odd people back at base. Martin and I had done everything ourselves: sorting out accommodation when we arrived at each destination; checking the weather each day; making the key go/no-go decisions that would determine whether we lived or died.

I stood watching as his car pulled away, and with that I was on my own. I'd spent six days crammed into a tiny glass bubble with the guy, flying over some of the most dangerous and inhospitable landscapes on the planet. But now it was up to me to finish the adventure alone.

20
HOME STRAIGHT

As I lifted off, going through the motions that had become so familiar to me over the past few days, I did some quick maths in my head. To be on the safe side, I wanted to touch down and land by half an hour after sunset, at the latest. That gave me roughly three and a half hours to make it down to Derbyshire, where I planned on landing at my ninety-year-old dad's place for the night. I wanted to surprise him and tell him all about my adventure across the Atlantic in a glass bubble.

The timings would have been touch-and-go even if I hadn't already been flying for six and a half hours that day. That made it one of the longest flying days of the trip – all that time sitting nearly totally still, with only hands and feet making slight adjustments to keep the machine in the air. It was hugely taxing – and it would be even more taxing to carry on alone, but there was no time to rest.

When I reached my desired altitude, I pushed south

on full throttle; full speed, hurtling down towards my dad's home in the beautiful Derbyshire dales.

Although I was making good progress, it was getting darker and darker, much faster than I'd anticipated. Soon I could see fog coming down, my visibility closing in with each passing minute.

Please, not fog – not now. This was the last thing I needed.

I checked the navigation system. I was heading for the Pennines, so the land was now rising up substantially. As I lifted the helicopter with it, I was getting closer and closer to the fog. If the fog came down, and the ground rose up, I would go into the fog – a helicopter pilot's worst nightmare – and be in real trouble.

I was hoping I'd be able to squeeze through, nipping over the tops of the Pennines before the cloud came too low. But it was a huge risk.

I continued full throttle southwards as the light faded. I can do this, I thought. I'll just be able to make it in time.

The problem was, I was also beginning to feel very tired. With nobody to talk to, nobody to help keep my spirits up, the energy really sapped out of me quickly.

Then, through a gap in the cloud layer, I saw the Pennines ahead of me. The land was rising up much more dramatically now – great big massive lumps of land – and it was coming up to kiss the fog. I knew, instantly, that there was no way that I was going to get through. The low light level, the fog and the high terrain all added up to make this a suicide mission.

I couldn't see anything. If there were any power lines, I would hit them. This was madness.

It struck me that it wasn't worth the risk, and that was OK; better an old pilot than a bold pilot. I just needed a Plan B.

I looked at the navigation system, clicking the button to show me the nearest helipads. A whole load of options came up. That, at least, was good.

It was now dark. It had gone nine o'clock and the sun had set. I needed to find somewhere I could stay – a hotel, whatever – but one that also had a helipad where I could land this thing.

I cycled through the various options my navigation system suggested. Not that one – it's too far from anything; not that one – it's a commercial airport. I weeded out the no-goers and only one possibility remained. At the same time, I was trying to keep an eye on the ground outside and the fog, which were both closing in fast. The visibility was terrible and I could just see the red rear lights of cars below me through the rain.

The remaining option was a place called Farlam Hall in Cumbria. Just west of the Pennines, it was only a 20-minute diversion from my current position. I could land on their helipad at the hall, get a nice kip and hopefully some good food, then be ready to go again in the morning. I looked up the phone number and called it, asking for permission to land. They said it was fine. Now I just needed to find the helipad.

I changed direction gingerly, continuing to navigate tentatively in the dark and the rain. I approached the village of Farlam with the fog looming above me. I was low enough that I could see the buildings, but high enough to avoid any potential disasters.

Which bloody house was Farlam Hall? I couldn't see a helipad anywhere.

Right. Let's think. Find the hall first. It'll be the big house, undoubtedly. It's only a small village – it'll be the big house in the village.

I continued flying around in circles, conscious now of my level above the ground as well. Then I spied an imposing building with a number of cars parked outside it. That had to be the hall; it couldn't be anywhere else. Next step: find the helipad.

Most helipads are a giant H painted on the ground in a white circle, so that when you get near, even when it's dark, the lettering shines into the sky. You can put your landing lights on, projecting a beam down, and landing should be relatively simple.

Here, however, I'd done a big circle around the hall, 500ft off the ground, blades whirring. I must have been making quite a racket and confusing the residents. At that point, I was too tired to worry about that and I needed to get the helicopter safely on the ground. The light was fading fast. Was there a helipad in sight? No way. I couldn't find a thing. I did another lap; nothing.

Right. I needed to steady the helicopter, by setting it to an altitude where I could take a proper look down and get my bearings.

There was no helipad. Nothing in sight.

I didn't have time for this; I needed to put this thing down. There was a stone wall around the hotel. I'd just have to find a suitable spot beyond it.

I spotted a field to the east that seemed suitable, just over the wall from the hall, and headed towards it. I called the hotel and they said yes I was OK to land there. As I put my hand down to make sure the friction on the collective lever was off again for landing, I caught my finger on a little wire tag under the knob. I winced. It felt like a deep cut. I pulled my finger back to inspect the damage. Blood was already gushing from the skin, spilling down my hand and arm.

This was the last thing I needed. Not only was I knackered, not only was it dark and foggy, but now I was bleeding and couldn't really do anything about it. I'd kept the helicopter in pretty good nick throughout the trip, and here I was, at the last leg, bleeding all over the damned thing.

I shoved my hand in my pocket, trying my best not to bleed all over my trousers, and pulled out my handkerchief. Of course, my other hand was busy on the cyclic, keeping the helicopter in the air, so it was a one-handed operation to try and stop the blood flow.

I wrapped the handkerchief around my finger as best I could, wedging it against the collective to clamp and stem the bleeding. My finger throbbed and pulsed, but the handkerchief seemed to be doing the job.

I circled around the field – it was now completely dark and I was struggling to see the ground even with the landing lights on. I lowered the helicopter slowly down. Damn: uneven ground. I pulled back up off the ground and tried another area. I was now very tired, I couldn't see the ground properly and there was fog above me. I had to get this damn thing down. Now.

Moving farther down the field towards the road, I slowly lowered the collective lever again, bringing the front of the skids into contact with the ground. I then gently lowered the back of the skids. The helicopter rocked on the uneven surface and then stopped rocking. I lowered the collective a bit more… It felt good. The helicopter seemed to be stable, and now it was on the ground.

Breathing a sigh of relief, I switched to idle mode, slowing the blades. I waited two minutes then turned off the engine. The blades freewheeled wildly above my head. I waited for the revs to drop, then gradually pulled on the rotor brake. The blades quickly came to a stop.

When I stepped out of the helicopter, I found myself

standing in a boggy field – damn! I thought. Well, at least I'm down. I looked over at the wall and trees that separated me from the hotel. There didn't seem to be any way over the wall. I should go to the road. Then I realised there was a bog and a river separating me from the road, completely barring the route in that direction. The only other way was to walk up the steep, wet field and skirt right around the stone wall separating me from the hotel. But that was going to be at least 500 metres. It was now very dark and, for good measure, it was also raining.

I took out my phone and switched on its torch. I breathed heavily – the adrenaline had been running for so many hours. I grabbed my backpack, locked the helicopter and headed for the wall. After all this, I couldn't believe that I was going to have to climb over it.

I walked for some 20 metres through the wet grass. My feet were now soaking. I climbed over the barbed-wire fence at the edge of the field and arrived at the large stone wall. There was a tree I thought I could shimmy up to try to get over the 8ft wall surrounding Farlam Hall.

The absurdity of this situation wasn't lost on me. I had made it all this way, and now, right at the end, I couldn't even reach the hotel.

I made sure my backpack was securely strapped onto my back and shimmied up the tree. The wall was about three feet from the tree. I stretched my legs out and one foot touched the top of the wall. I tried to push off the tree but couldn't. I was wedged with one foot on the tree and one on the wall. I must look like a cat burglar – and not a particularly competent one. I pushed very hard on the tree and jumped, falling onto my hands and knees on top of the wall.

So far so good. I'm on top of the wall. Now, how the hell do I get down?

I crawled on my hands and knees along the top of the wall to a compost heap, which was 4ft high and next to the wall. What if it was all soft and I just sank into it? I decided I had had enough and I just wanted to get to the hotel and beg a room, so I was past caring. I jumped off the wall and hit the top of the compost heap. It was solid; there is a God. I walked down the heap into the gardeners' area, around the potting sheds and found my way out into the car park. Brushing off the mud, leaves and dirt from my trousers and shirt, I headed for the front door.

I stepped inside. There was nobody at the front desk. It looked very posh – like one of those old country-house hotels – and there was a great smell of cooking coming from somewhere. Oh, for a good steak now! I could feel the saliva juices kicking in.

There was a mirror on the wall so I checked how messy I was. Another quick brush-off and I ran my fingers through my hair. My bloodied finger was still wrapped in my handkerchief, I had oil on my hands, and was a bit hot and sticky from all the flying that day, but overall, not too bad, bearing in mind what I'd just been through. But this was a smart place, so I was still worried they might throw me out for being too scruffy. I walked down the corridor following the sign to the restaurant. I saw a woman carrying a tray.

'Any chance I can get a room for the night?' It was now 9.25pm.

She hesitated. 'I'll go and check.'

She disappeared into the restaurant with the tray and left me standing in the corridor. A few minutes later, she returned.

'I've spoken to the manager and yes, that's fine. You can have the Esmeralda suite.'

'Could I also get something to eat?'

'The kitchen shuts in five minutes.'

'I'm ready to order now.'

'I'll go and ask the chef.'

I was again left in the corridor.

'The chef said yes.'

'That's absolutely fantastic.'

'You'll need to go straight into the restaurant.'

She showed me in and I sat at a small table for two and put my bag down next to me. With its spotlights around the walls, white table cloths, and gleaming wine glasses, the restaurant was clearly fine dining. I ordered a steak.

'Would you like something to drink?' asked the waitress.

I was determined to celebrate my first night back on UK soil in style. 'I'd love a bottle of Châteauneuf-du-Pape, if you have it. Also, do you have a bandage?' My finger was still bleeding quite heavily.

'No problem.'

The wine and bandage arrived, and then my steak. I was in paradise, and with each sip of wine and mouthful of steak, I started to feel the energy coursing back into my veins. The only other diners were a table of three people close to me. There was an American woman and an older man and woman. They seemed to be very attentive to the American.

Later, the man came over to me and introduced himself as Jeremy. He ran the hotel, and the American lady was one of its investors who had just arrived from the States. I told him I had just landed in a helicopter and had flown across the Atlantic.

He was fascinated and invited me to join him for a drink in the bar. We sat chatting until gone midnight, with him telling me amusing stories about running a hotel, and me sharing some of my exploits in the helicopter.

Also, I had to ask: 'Where the hell is your helipad? I couldn't see it anywhere, so I ended up sticking it in the field next door. It was pretty boggy, though.'

My host laughed sheepishly. 'I had to move it from

its original place and the field where you landed is meant to be the helipad. I painted an H in the grass, but it's grown out, and we've had very heavy rain recently which is why the field is so waterlogged. I'm sorry it wasn't more obvious.'

I decided not to compound his embarrassment by mentioning my scramble over the wall and into the compost heap. And, privately, I could see the funny side of that absurd and undignified return to English soil.

In the morning, Jeremy asked if he could see the helicopter. After I'd packed my bag, we headed out to the helicopter, going the long way around on the road, so no walls to climb this time.

'Beautiful machine,' he said. 'I can't believe you have flown all that way in this.'

He jumped up into the cockpit and sat in the captain's seat. We chatted for a few minutes while I carried out all the flight checks – and got very soggy feet into the bargain. My checks done, Jeremy got out, I jumped in and he wished me a safe journey.

I lifted into the air, aware of him filming me on his phone as I departed.

Next stop Guernsey. Fingers crossed.

Although I had really been hoping to see my dad, I realised I would not be able both to visit him and get back to Guernsey within the day. So, I set my course for the Channel Islands.

As I approached the south coast of England, I tried calling up Bournemouth, but there was no answer. This struck me as strange – I tried another local frequency and the same thing happened. Nobody seemed to be answering. Maybe there weren't many air traffic controllers working because of Covid, I thought.

I skirted around Bournemouth's controlled airspace and headed out across the English Channel towards Guernsey. Checking the radio again, I realised I had accidentally knocked the volume knob very low, so it was no wonder I couldn't hear Bournemouth. I turned up the volume and tuned into the London Information service that covers most of the UK.

I like speaking to the London Information guys when I'm crossing the Channel because their antennae have a great range, so if I have a problem I can instantly communicate it to them. Most other services don't reach as far as the Channel Islands, but I can speak to London Information all the way to the Channel Islands boundary and then switch to Jersey Control to take me into Channel Islands waters.

I'd been flying for nearly three hours, and the fuel gauge was beginning to look low, although the weather and visibility were good. It was actually a nice flying day – and after seven days flying over iceberg-infested seas, it was wonderful to be able to finish the journey in this way. I couldn't wait to see Steph and Liz.

HOME STRAIGHT

As I approached Guernsey, I was switched over to the island's approach and then to its control tower. Guernsey is a beautiful lump of rock out in the English Channel, just 65km from the French coast. It is covered in greenhouses, and the sun glinted and flashed off their glass panels, at times creating a blinding display of light as I came in. My low-fuel light was about to come on – time to get the helicopter on the ground.

The tower cleared me for runway 27 and I brought the helicopter in smoothly, exiting taxiway Alpha and dropping down onto the tarmac.

I had done it! Canada to Guernsey – 4,300 miles by helicopter in eight days! The helicopter was in one piece – and so, amazingly enough, was I. I got out of the cabin, tired but happy, and saw my friend, waiting to receive his new toy, waving at me beside the tower. I waved back.

As I strolled towards him, the whole of my adventure flashed before me: the first glimpse of the helicopter in the hangar at the Bell factory in Mirabel; the Inuit girl in the shop in Pangnirtung who was desperate to escape to Europe for a different kind of life; and breaking into the hotel in the freezing early morning and being questioned by the police. I'd flown over icy seas with red warning lights flashing and beeping, and Martin and me thinking it was curtains. I'd stood in the eerie silence of the polar ice cap, feeling a sense of privilege and awe as I gazed in amazement at the incredible landscape. I'd also found myself being filmed by Reynir, flying perilously close to me in thick fog after taking off from Reykjavik. I'd seen the beautiful green Faroe Isles, and I'd had a rollercoaster flight across the Highlands of Scotland. And, of course, I couldn't forget Roberto, that generous and gentle soul in Greenland. Every time I drank a glass of good Italian wine I would think of him.

While I didn't see any polar bears, the trip had allowed me to observe how the Inuit people manage to survive in one of the remotest regions on earth. It had been a glimpse of another world, so far removed from our lives in the West, where we can do so many things by just tapping the keyboard on our phone or computer. We take all this for granted. It was sobering to realise that's not how everyone on our planet lives.

I had certainly put the 505 through her paces – and she had come up trumps all the way. I would be sorry to say goodbye to her, but I could certainly assure my friend that his decision to buy this helicopter had been a good one.

The trip had indeed been a crazy idea – and a crazy experience. But sometimes in life we need to do something crazy.

ACKNOWLEDGEMENTS

I would like to thank my brother, my dad and my two daughters, Steph and Lizzie. Although they all think I'm mad, I am always certain of their love. On adventures like this one – in my lonely, scared moments – this is a never-ending source of strength and comfort spurring me on to the finish.

I would also like to thank Nick Russell, who, early on, helped me enormously to pull everything together. Nick, thank you so much; without you I don't think I would have got this book over the line!

Thanks also to Dan Hiscocks at Eye Books, my editors Clio Mitchell, Greg Watts and Simon Edge, and to Dan Roberts; to Adrian Bleese for his helpful comments; to Alexis Baird at Bell for help with the cover image; and to Andy Watts at Bell for going above and beyond and flying out to Iceland to service the helicopter midway through my adventure – a legal requirement without which I would not have been able to carry on.

This book is a true story of an incredible adventure to be the first person to fly a Bell 505 helicopter across the Atlantic. While great care has been taken in the book's production, some parts are enhanced for the reader's enjoyment.

Also by Jules Mountain

Aftershock

One man's quest and the quake on Everest

When the worst earthquake to hit Nepal in living memory strikes on 25 April 2015, Jules Mountain is shivering in his tent at Base Camp.

To reach the summit of Everest has been a life-long dream, one which he is more determined than ever to realise, having won his battle with cancer two years earlier.

The climbers are faced with an impossible set of decisions: to get to a safe zone as quickly as possible? To try to be of assistance in the relief effort? To push on despite everything? All three options have huge implications – moral and logistical – and Jules' unique situation sets him apart from the rest.

This is the true story of one man's ordeal during the most deadly disaster in the history of mountaineering on Everest, which would leave over 8,000 dead and thousands more missing and injured; how logic, compassion and risk assessment are affected by altitude, vested interests and the stress of extreme circumstances.

While very few of us will ever find ourselves in Jules' boots, Aftershock throws up questions which transfer surprisingly well back to everyday modern life.

'A remarkable chronicle of resilience and resourcefulness'
Daily Mail

If you have enjoyed *Arctic Insanity*, do please help us spread the word – by putting a review online; by posting something on social media; or in the old-fashioned way by simply telling your friends or family about it.

Book publishing is a very competitive business these days, in a saturated market, and small independent publishers such as ourselves are often crowded out by the big houses. Support from readers like you can make all the difference to a book's success.

Many thanks.
Dan Hiscocks
Founder, Eye Books